Five-Minute art IDEAS

print SCISSORS GLUE paint

Edited by
**Paul Harrison, Nicola Wright and
Helen Burnford**

Designed by
**Nicky Chapman,
Chris Dymond and
Kate Buxton**

Illustrated by
**Clare Beaton,
Lynn Farmer and
Chris Dymond**

zigzag

Contents

print

Contents

Hints and Tips

Before you begin making any of the ideas in this book, put on old clothes so that it won't matter if you get messy.

Keep some scrap paper handy for trying out your prints before you use your good paper.

Cover your work area with old newspapers before you start in case anything spills.

Always ask an adult to help when using sharp objects such as craft knives. You can buy round-ended safety scissors from most craft shops.

There are many different types of paint you can use to make your prints. Poster paint is one of the best.

It is a good idea to keep pieces of scrap paper, cloth, and other bits and pieces you have collected in a box. Then they will be ready to use when you need them.

There are lots of different types of glue that can be used to stick objects to blocks or cardboard so you can print with them. A craft glue is one of the best to use, unless the directions say otherwise.

Remember to rinse your brushes after using them and to clean up afterward!

5

Handy Prints

You need

Liquid paint

Scissors

Glue

Craft paper

Plate

1

Pour some paint on a plate. Place your hand in the paint, and then press your hand down on the craft paper.

2

Make lots of hand prints in different colors.

3

When the paint is dry, cut around each hand shape.

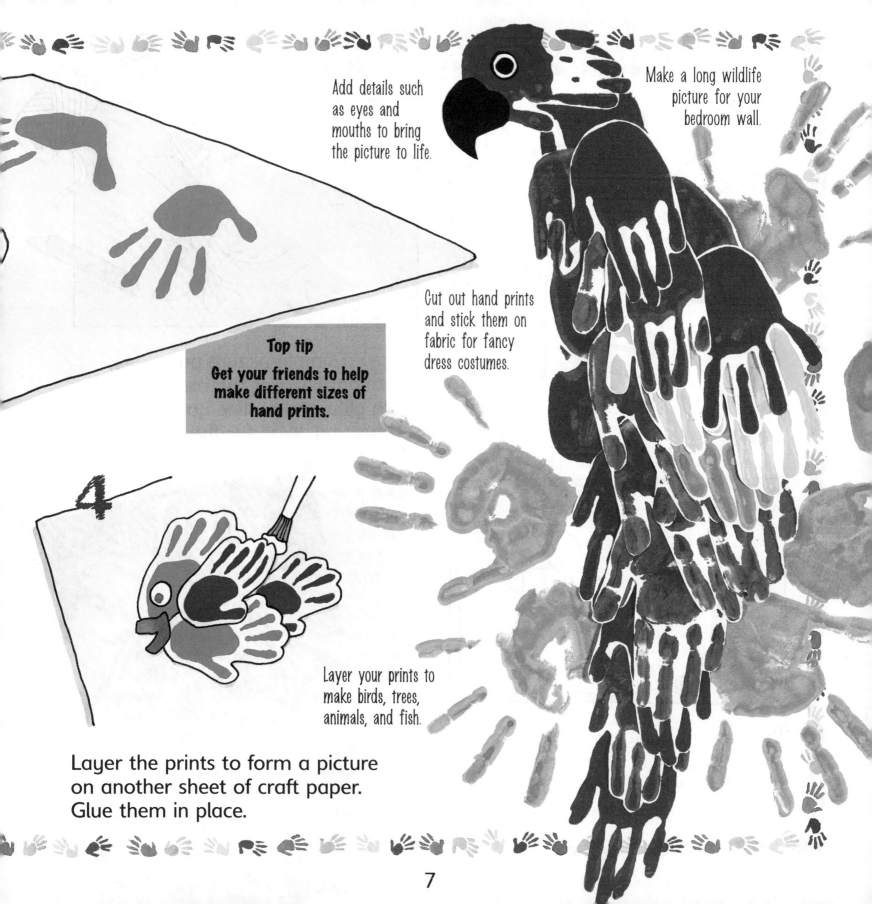

Add details such as eyes and mouths to bring the picture to life.

Make a long wildlife picture for your bedroom wall.

Cut out hand prints and stick them on fabric for fancy dress costumes.

Top tip

Get your friends to help make different sizes of hand prints.

Layer your prints to make birds, trees, animals, and fish.

Layer the prints to form a picture on another sheet of craft paper. Glue them in place.

String Prints

You need

Cotton string

Thick cardboard

Glue

Liquid paint

Brush

Ink roller

Colored paper

1 Draw a simple picture on thick cardboard. Cover the cardboard with glue and outline your drawing with string. Wait for the glue to dry.

2 Brush paint thinly and evenly onto the string. Lay paper over the top and roll over the back of it with an ink roller. Peel the paper back carefully.

Instead of an ink roller, you could use a rolling pin or soda bottle.

Use your printed paper for wrapping gifts. Make a card and gift tag to match.

For another kind of print, cut two 4-inch (10-cm) squares from the cardboard. Make marks every 1/2 inch (1 cm) down the sides. Draw wavy lines to link the dots.

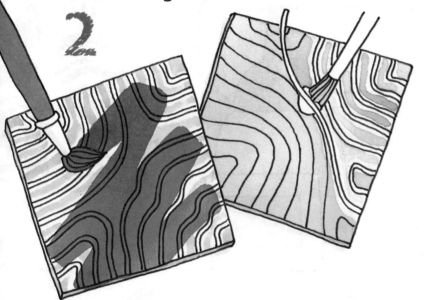

Glue string over the lines. Let it dry, and cover with paint as before.

Roll over the back with a roller.

Press one square down in a corner of a sheet of paper. Line the other square up to the first and print again. Then print the first one again, and so on, until the sheet is covered.

Odds and Ends

You need

Everyday objects from around the house

Liquid paint

Paper

Plates

1

Find small objects around the house that have interesting shapes and flat surfaces. Ask an adult if the objects you have chosen are all right to use.

2

Put some different colors of paint into plates.

Dip your object into the paint and then press it down firmly on a sheet of paper. Build up a pattern by using different shapes and colors.

Cork

Rubber band

Bottle cap

Clothespin

Fork

Pencil eraser

Top tip

If the objects you use are needed again, use a water-base paint that can be washed off.

Sticky Prints

You need

Smooth, wipeable surface

Thick paste glue

Powdered paint

Newspaper

Paper

1 Put one color of paint on one side of the glue and another color on the other side for a multicolor print.

Place a dollop of glue in the center of a smooth, wipeable surface. Add a small spoonful of powdered paint to the glue.

2 Mix together the powdered paint and glue with your finger. Spread the mixture thinly over the surface.

3 Draw a pattern or shape in the mixture, using thick, wide lines. Place a sheet of paper over it. Then lay a piece of newspaper over the top.

Press the newspaper down hard, smoothing across the whole surface.

Remove the newspaper and then carefully peel off the paper, starting at one corner. Let it dry.

Top tip

Make a pattern, such as water, to use as a background. Then glue an animal or other shape on top to make a picture.

If you draw a shape in the glue, you can cut it out and stick it on top of a pattern.

13

Veggie **P**rints

You need

Fruit and vegetables

Liquid paint

Thick paper

Plates

2

Put different colors of paint in plates. Dip the pieces of fruit and vegetables in the paint.

1

Ask an adult to cut up the fruit and vegetables for you. Try cutting different shapes into them.

Mushroom (without stalk)

Broccoli head

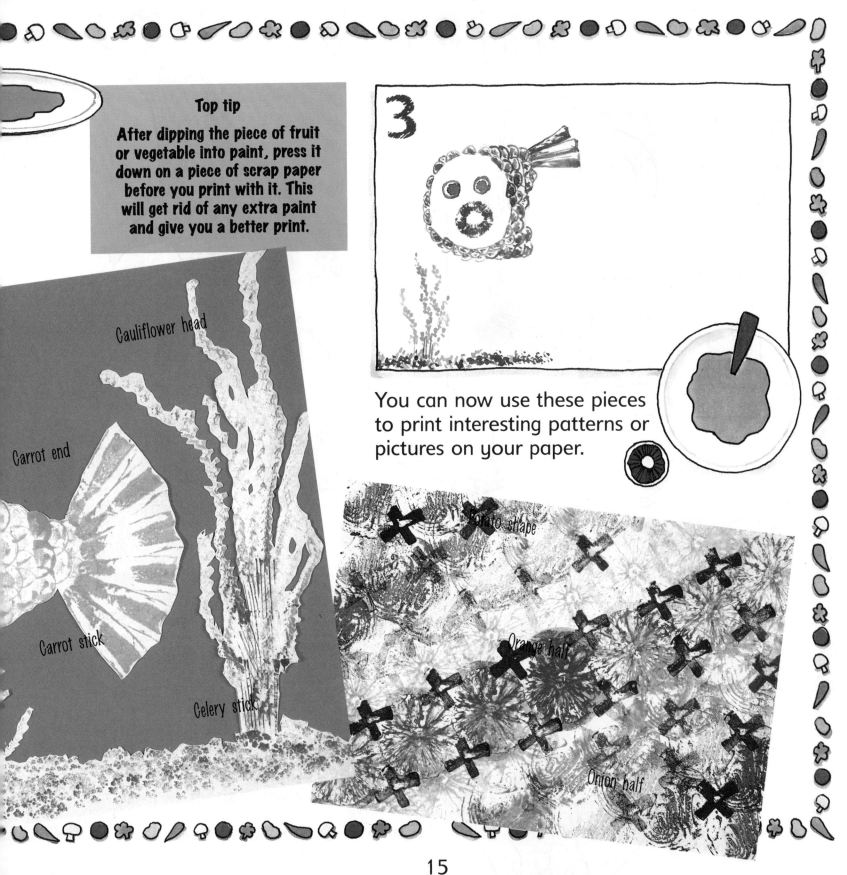

Top tip

After dipping the piece of fruit or vegetable into paint, press it down on a piece of scrap paper before you print with it. This will get rid of any extra paint and give you a better print.

3

Cauliflower head

Carrot end

Carrot stick

Celery stick

You can now use these pieces to print interesting patterns or pictures on your paper.

Potato shape

Orange half

Onion half

15

Rag Printing

You need

Rags

Plate

Scissors

Liquid paint

Paper

Rubber bands

Printing with the closed or the open end of the rag will give you different effects.

1 Twist and scrunch up a rag. Wrap a rubber band around it tightly to hold the shape together.

2 Put some paint in a plate. Dip the end of the rag into the paint and lightly dab it over a sheet of paper.

3

Use other rags to print with different colors.

4

When the paint is dry, turn the paper over and draw shapes. Cut them out and stick them together to make pictures.

Block Printing

You need

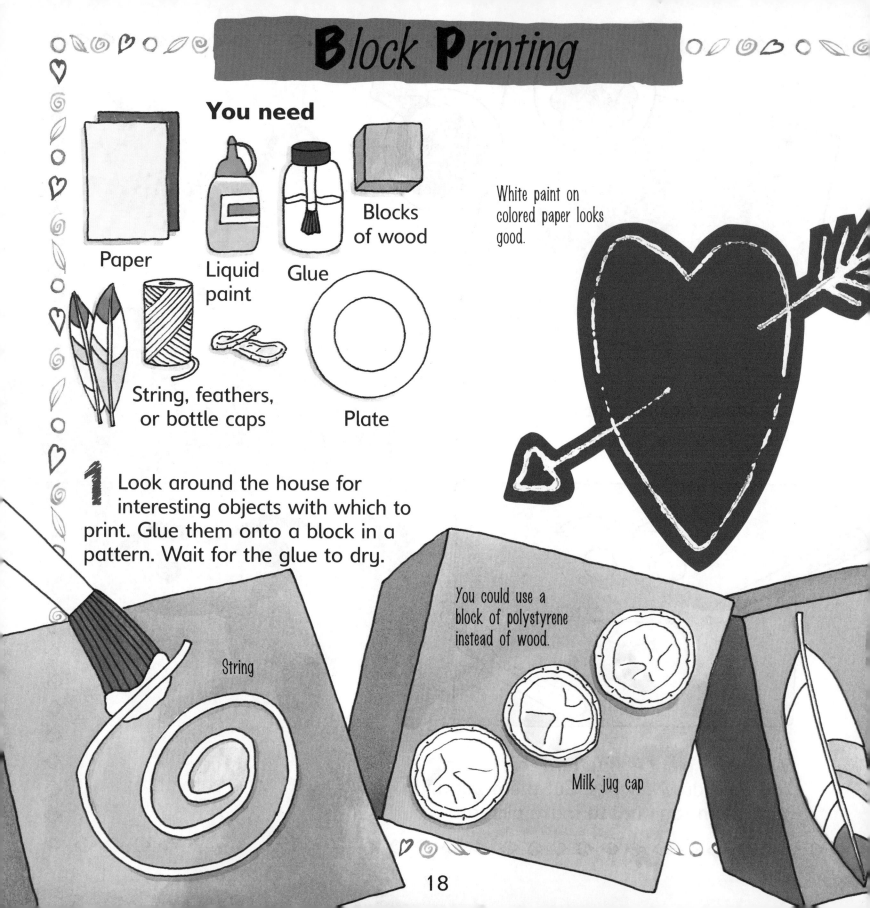

Paper

Liquid paint

Glue

Blocks of wood

String, feathers, or bottle caps

Plate

White paint on colored paper looks good.

1 Look around the house for interesting objects with which to print. Glue them onto a block in a pattern. Wait for the glue to dry.

String

You could use a block of polystyrene instead of wood.

Milk jug cap

2 Pour some paint in a plate. Press the patterned side of the block into the paint and then onto paper.

Top tip

Press objects into a block of clay and then remove. Press the block into paint and then onto paper. The shape of the object will show up as white.

Feather

Marbling

You need

Baking pan

Oil-base paint

Water

Turpentine Vinegar Brush Paper

1

Fill a baking pan almost to
the rim with water. Add a few drops
of vinegar to the water.

2 Now mix your paint with some
turpentine to make it thin and
drop small amounts of different
colored paints into
the water.

3

Lay a sheet of paper on the water. Wait a couple of seconds and then lift it off.

4 Let the paper dry and you will see your marbled effect.

Use the paper to wrap gifts, or cut shapes out of it and stick them on poster board to make pictures.

Top tip

If you put wallpaper paste into the water as well as vinegar, your pattern will set even better.

You need

Paper

Liquid paint

Plastic adhesive

Baking pan

String

Rolling pin

1 Tie a piece of string to one end of a rolling pin or cardboard tube. Wind the string tightly around it until you reach the other end and tie the string again.

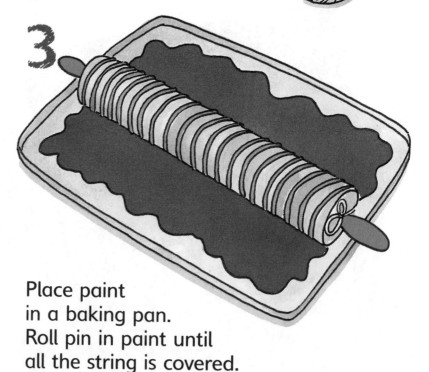

2 Tear or cut shapes out of paper. Stick the shapes on a piece of paper with a little plastic adhesive.

3

Place paint in a baking pan. Roll pin in paint until all the string is covered.

You can do lots of different things using the rolling pin. Paint a tiger, leaving out the stripes. Then go over it with the rolling pin and it will look like a tiger in long grass.

4

Roll over the shapes again in a different direction to create a checked pattern.

Roll over the paper and the shapes. When the paint is dry, peel off the shapes.

Use the shapes to make pictures.

Pizza Prints

You need

Sheet of polystyrene (for example, a pizza base)

Brush

Paper

Pencil

Liquid paint

Plate

Draw deeper lines for your main outline.

1 Draw a shape lightly on a sheet of polystyrene. Once you are happy with it, go over the lines again, pressing down hard so that an indented line is made.

Draw shallower lines for details such as fur and faces.

2

Quickly paint over the whole surface and then press it facedown on a sheet of paper.

Don't use too much paint and try not to get it in the lines.

Top tip

Wipe off your polystyrene with a damp cloth before printing with another color.

More Ideas

Use your thumbs and fingers to create different pictures.

You need an ink stamp pad.

Complete your picture by adding details with a pen.

Read and find out how to make creepy critters, fantastic finger puppets, and other great ideas using glue.

GLUE

Contents

Hints and Tips

There are lots of different types of paint that you can use to decorate your art ideas, but using felt-tip pens or colored pencils is a quicker way of coloring things.

Cover your work area with old newspapers before you start in case anything spills.

Always ask an adult for help when using sharp objects such as craft knives. You can buy round-ended safety scissors at most craft shops.

Put on old clothes before you start working so you won't splash your good clothes with glue or paint.

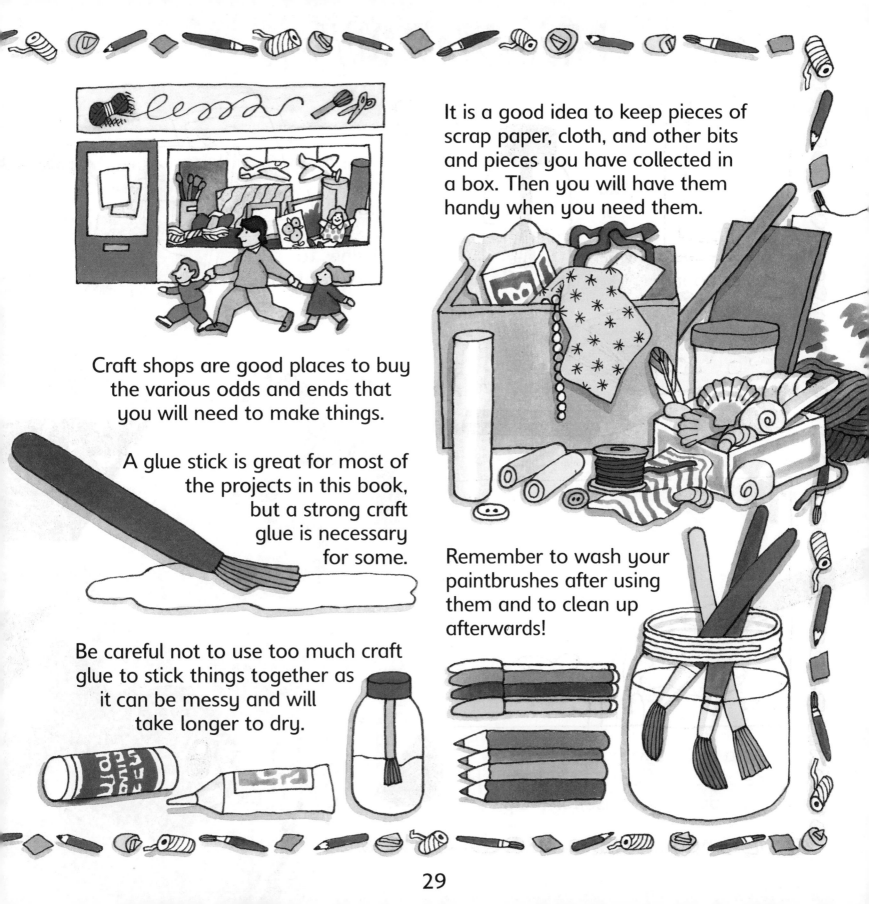

Craft shops are good places to buy the various odds and ends that you will need to make things.

A glue stick is great for most of the projects in this book, but a strong craft glue is necessary for some.

Be careful not to use too much craft glue to stick things together as it can be messy and will take longer to dry.

It is a good idea to keep pieces of scrap paper, cloth, and other bits and pieces you have collected in a box. Then you will have them handy when you need them.

Remember to wash your paintbrushes after using them and to clean up afterwards!

Magazine Collage

You need

Poster board

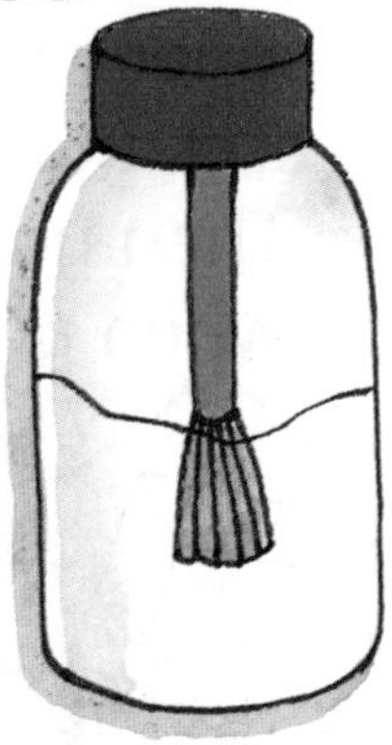

Glue or glue stick

Color magazines

Pencil

2 Look through color magazines to find pictures with the colors you want.

1 Draw a picture with a pencil on a piece of poster board. Decide which colors you want to use for the picture.

3

Tear the pictures into small pieces and sort the pieces into piles, a different color in each pile.

4

Now glue the torn magazine pieces onto the poster board. Use the picture drawn in pencil as a guide.

Caterpillar

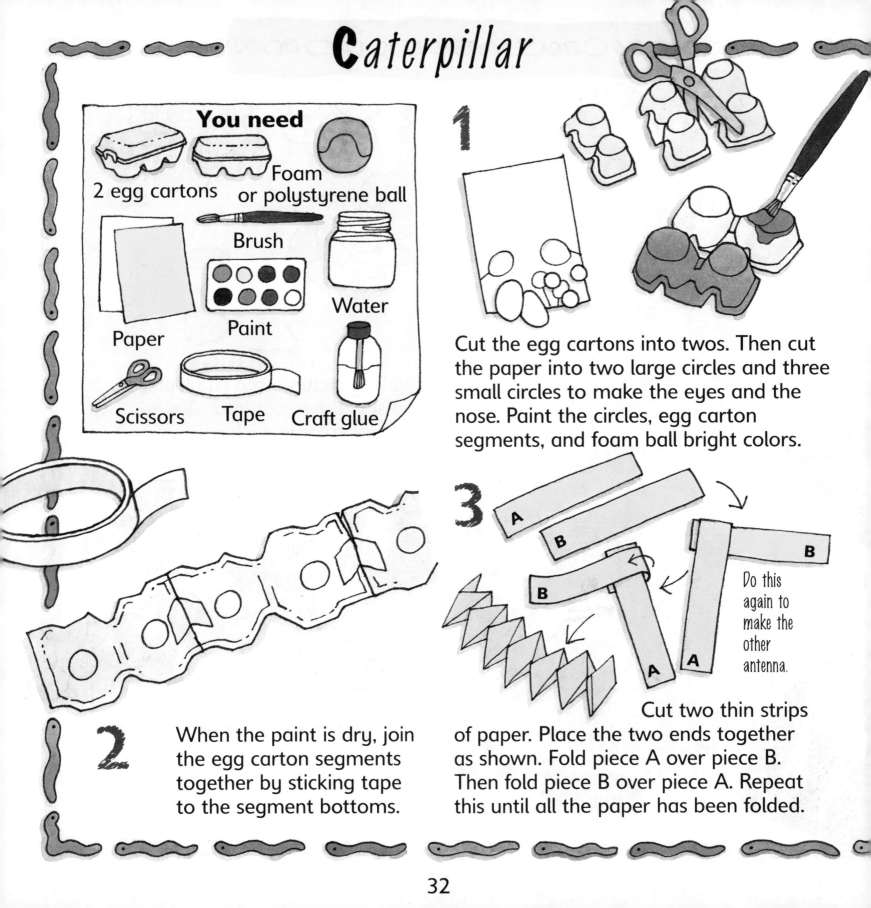

You need

2 egg cartons

Foam or polystyrene ball

Brush

Paint

Water

Paper

Scissors

Tape

Craft glue

1 Cut the egg cartons into twos. Then cut the paper into two large circles and three small circles to make the eyes and the nose. Paint the circles, egg carton segments, and foam ball bright colors.

2 When the paint is dry, join the egg carton segments together by sticking tape to the segment bottoms.

3 Cut two thin strips of paper. Place the two ends together as shown. Fold piece A over piece B. Then fold piece B over piece A. Repeat this until all the paper has been folded.

A

B

B

B

A

A

Do this again to make the other antenna.

4

You can paint dots or squiggles on the body of your caterpillar.

Glue the eyes and the antennae to the side of the foam ball. Then glue the ball to the egg carton body.

Glue the small circles onto the large circles to make the eyes.

Use the third circle to make the nose.

Top tip
Try putting the small circles in different positions on the large circles to give your caterpillar different expressions.

33

Finger Puppets

You need

Paper

Felt-tip pens

Glue or glue stick

Pencil

Scissors

1

Draw a triangle with a rounded bottom on a piece of paper. Cut it out and glue the sides together to form a cone.

Remember to make the puppet big enough to get your finger into!

2

Draw and cut out ears, whiskers, and a tail and glue these to the cone. Draw dots for eyes.

3

To make a different kind of finger puppet, fold a piece of paper in half and draw a picture on it. Draw a small tab on the open side of the paper. Color your picture.

4

Cut the picture out, fold the tabs in, and glue the tabs together.

Glitter Pictures

You need

Colored poster board

Sand or glitter

Pencil

Glue or glue stick

1 Draw a picture on a piece of colored poster board.

2 Go over your picture with glue. Gently sprinkle your glitter or sand onto the poster board.

3

Let the glue dry for a few minutes. Then tip the loose glitter or sand onto newspaper.

String Snails

You need

String

Scissors

Craft glue

Felt or poster board

Pencil

Sequins or beads

1 Cut string into pieces 10 inches (25 cm) long, and coil them to make snail shells.

2 Draw the snails' bodies on the pieces of felt or poster board and cut them out.

3 Glue the shells to the bodies and glue on small sequins or beads for eyes.

4

Cut short lengths of string for "feelers" and glue on the sides of the heads.

Top tip

Make a plant out of string and felt for your snails to sit on.

Pasta Pictures

You need

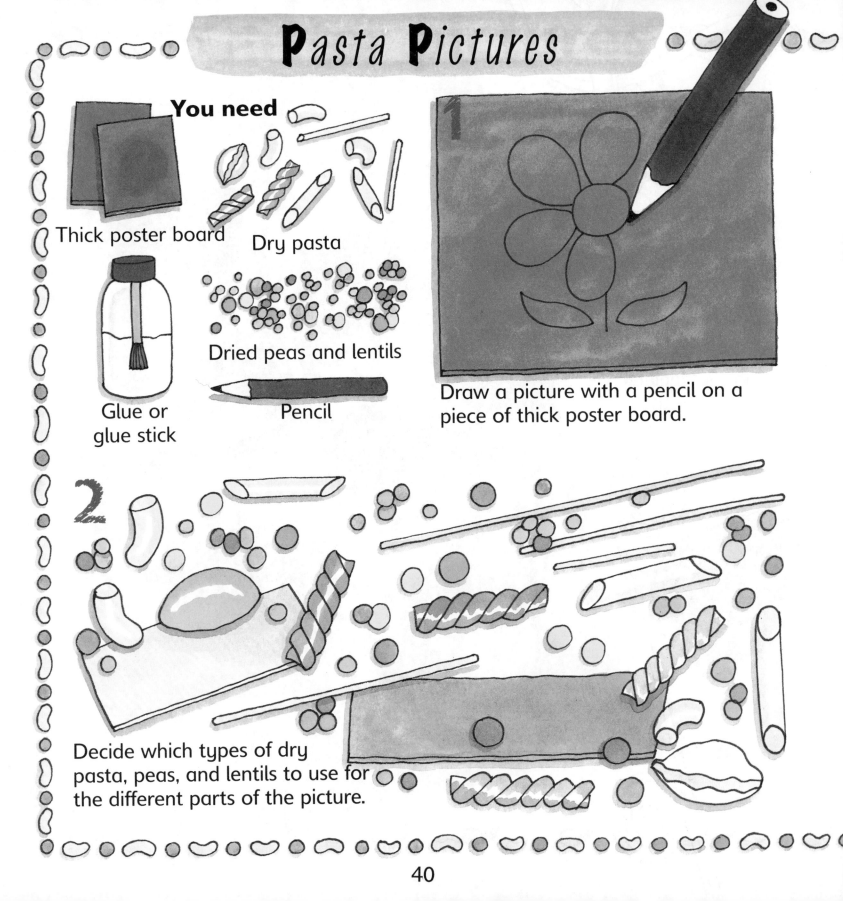

Thick poster board

Dry pasta

Glue or glue stick

Dried peas and lentils

Pencil

1 Draw a picture with a pencil on a piece of thick poster board.

2 Decide which types of dry pasta, peas, and lentils to use for the different parts of the picture.

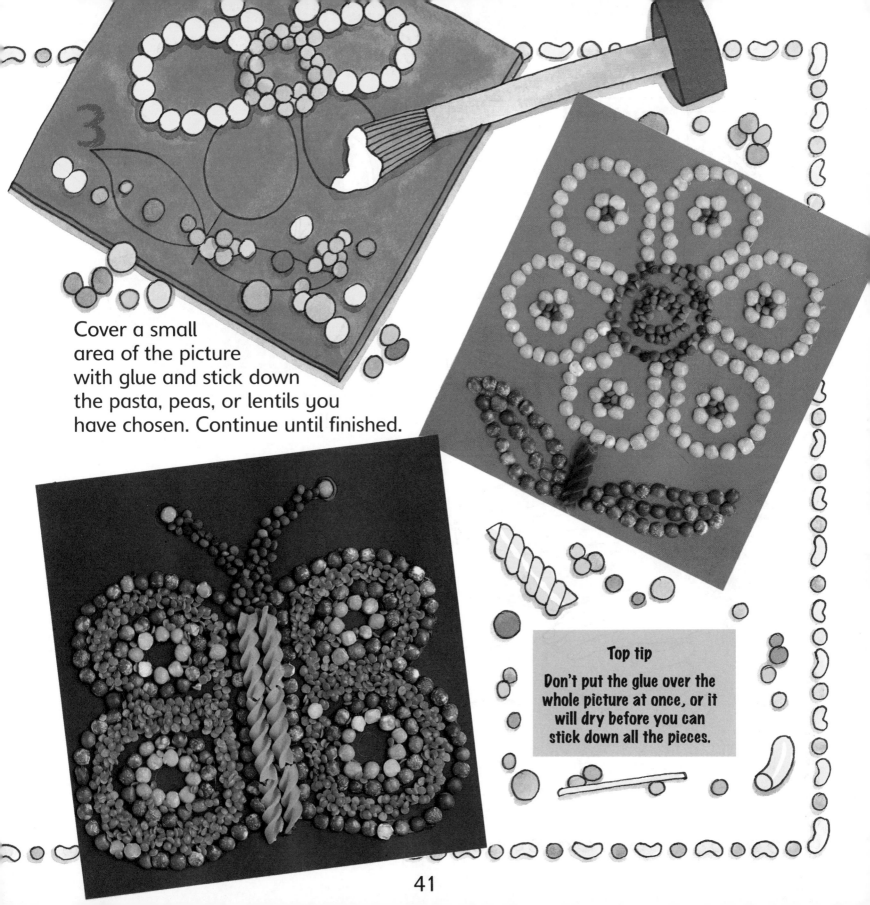

Cover a small area of the picture with glue and stick down the pasta, peas, or lentils you have chosen. Continue until finished.

Top tip

Don't put the glue over the whole picture at once, or it will dry before you can stick down all the pieces.

41

Jewelry

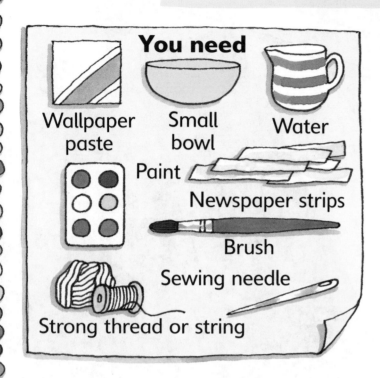

You need

Wallpaper paste

Small bowl

Water

Paint

Newspaper strips

Brush

Sewing needle

Strong thread or string

1

Put the paste in a small bowl and add a little water.

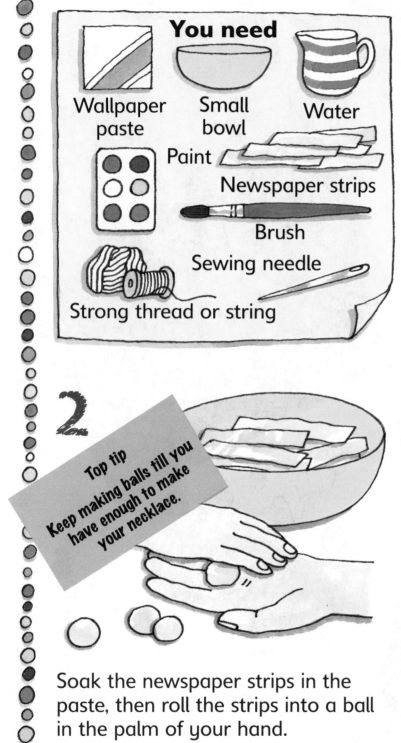

2

Top tip
Keep making balls till you have enough to make your necklace.

Soak the newspaper strips in the paste, then roll the strips into a ball in the palm of your hand.

3

Ask an adult to put the balls into an oven at a low temperature (on "warm" or 200°) until they are dry.

4

Top tip
Put each ball on top of a piece of modeling clay before pushing the needle through. This will stop the needle from damaging the table.

Paint each ball. When dry, push a threaded needle through the center of each ball. When all the balls are threaded on the string, tie the two ends together to form a necklace.

Fabric Fish

You need

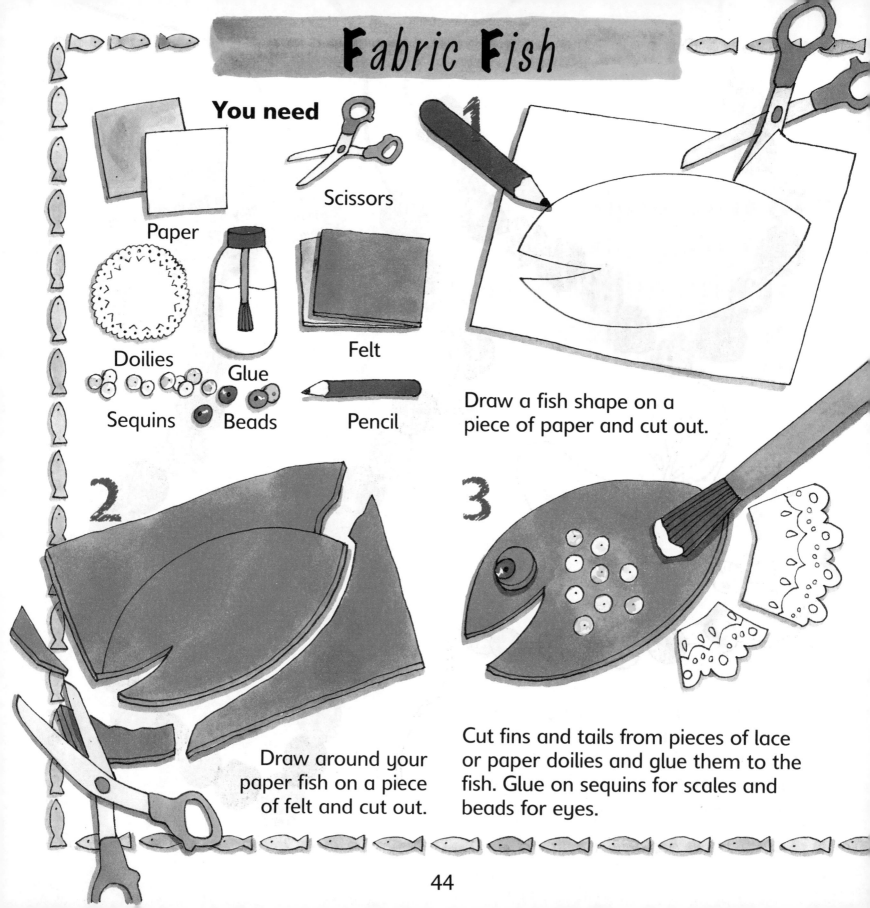

Paper

Scissors

Doilies

Glue

Felt

Sequins

Beads

Pencil

1 Draw a fish shape on a piece of paper and cut out.

2 Draw around your paper fish on a piece of felt and cut out.

3 Cut fins and tails from pieces of lace or paper doilies and glue them to the fish. Glue on sequins for scales and beads for eyes.

Top tip
Make a bowl for your fish out of a round piece of colored poster board. Use pipe cleaners for weeds and sequins for bubbles.

You need

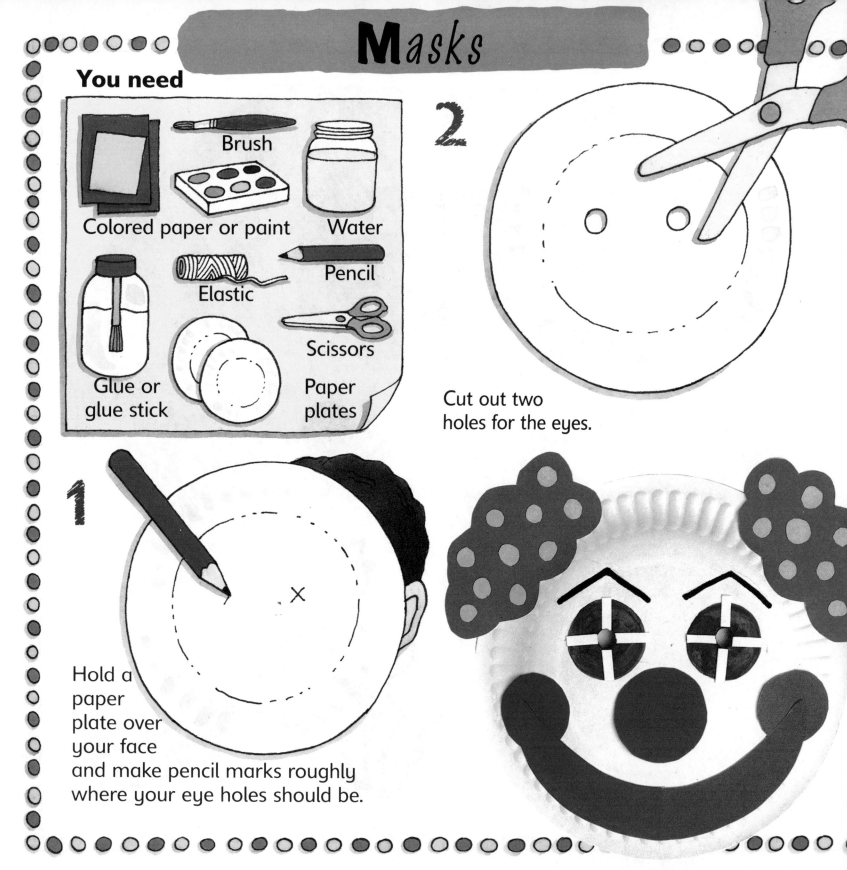

Brush

Colored paper or paint

Water

Elastic

Pencil

Glue or glue stick

Scissors

Paper plates

1 Hold a paper plate over your face and make pencil marks roughly where your eye holes should be.

2 Cut out two holes for the eyes.

3

Use paint
or pieces of
colored paper to make a face.

Top tip

Ask a friend to tighten the
elastic while you are
wearing the mask so that it
stays on.

4

Make two
small holes
on either side
of the mask and thread the elastic
through. Make sure it is tight enough
before knotting on both sides.

You can make this excellent ugly bug by using the head from the caterpillar you made on page 32.

Glue another foam ball to the head to make a body and glue bendy straps to the body to make the legs.

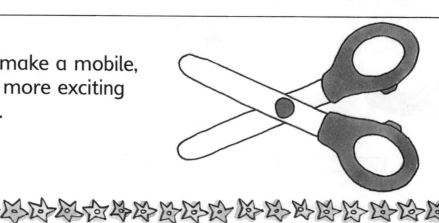

You can turn your bug into a spider by giving it eight legs instead of six. Don't forget to remove the antennae!

Try making papier-mâché jewelry in exciting shapes, like this star pendant. Make the pendant in the same way as the balls on page 42.

Decorate the jewelry with paint and glitter.

Rather than roll the papier-mâché into balls, form it into any shape you want.

Now discover how to make a mobile, pop-up cards and lots more exciting projects using scissors.

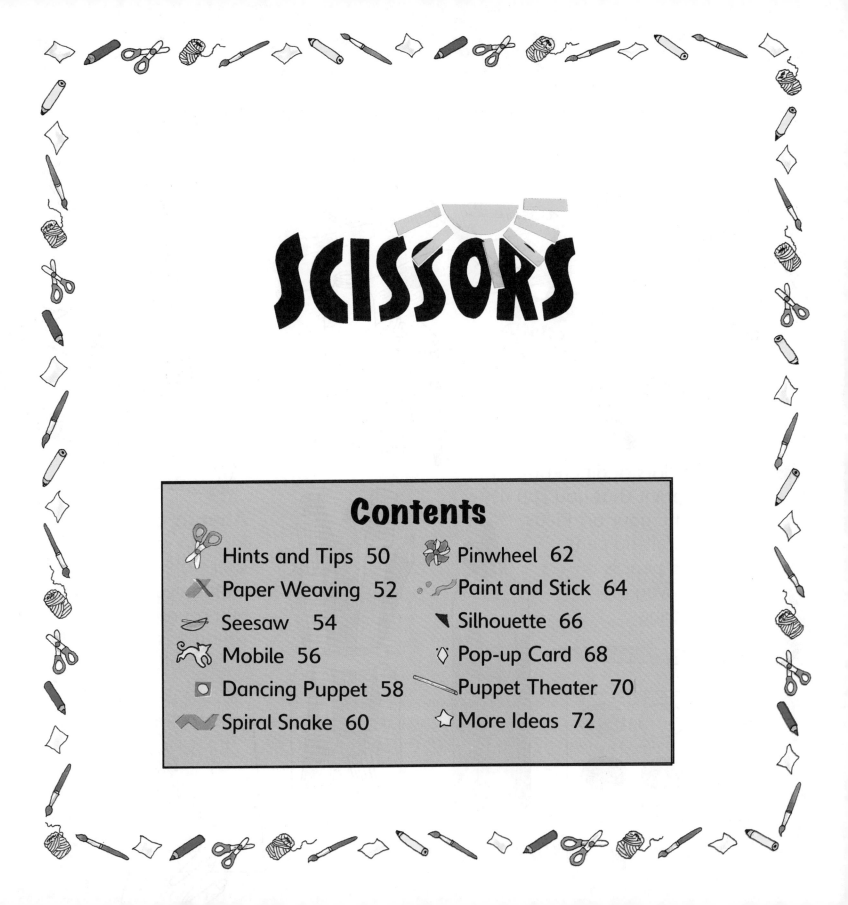

SCISSORS

Contents

Hints and Tips

It is a good idea to cover your work area with newspaper before you start in case anything spills.

Put on old clothes before you start working.

There are lots of different types of paint that you can use to decorate your art ideas, but using felt-tip pens or colored pencils is a quicker way of coloring things.

Always ask an adult for help when using sharp objects such as craft knives. You can buy round-ended safety scissors at most craft shops.

Craft shops are good places to buy the various odds and ends that you will need to make things.

You can get thin pieces of wire with eyelets from craft shops. These are ideal for attaching thread to your mobile so you can hang it.

You can use most types of glue to make the things in this book. However, a craft glue is one of the best types to use, unless the instructions say otherwise.

It is a good idea to keep pieces of scrap paper, cloth, and other bits and pieces you have collected in a box. Then you will have them handy when you need to use them.

Remember to clean up!

You need

Scissors

Colored paper

Strips of colored paper

1

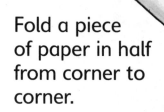

Fold a piece of paper in half from corner to corner.

2

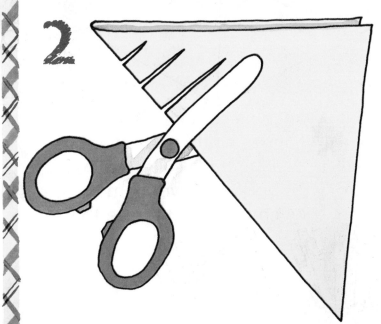

Cut a row of slits along the folded edge.

3

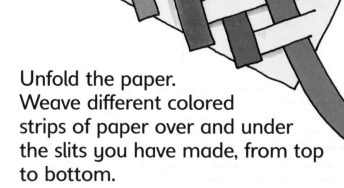

Unfold the paper. Weave different colored strips of paper over and under the slits you have made, from top to bottom.

To get diagonal stripes, fold and cut the paper as before. Then weave different colored strips through the paper as shown.

53

Seesaw

You need

Poster board

Compass

Pencil

Scissors

Paint

Brush

Water

Glue

Paper fasteners

1 Draw a large circle, a large rectangle, and a small rectangle on the poster board and cut out. Paint the pieces and let them dry.

2 Make a zigzag fold on the small rectangle and fold the circle in half.

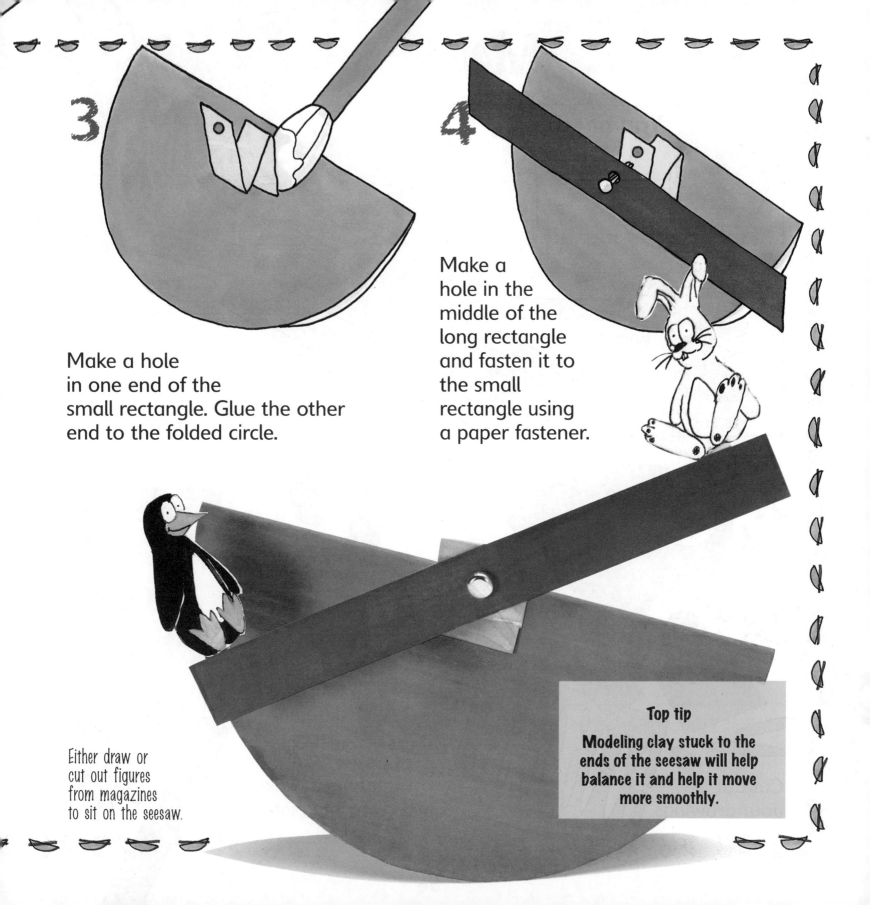

3

Make a hole in one end of the small rectangle. Glue the other end to the folded circle.

4

Make a hole in the middle of the long rectangle and fasten it to the small rectangle using a paper fastener.

Either draw or cut out figures from magazines to sit on the seesaw.

Top tip

Modeling clay stuck to the ends of the seesaw will help balance it and help it move more smoothly.

Mobile

You need

Colored poster board

Glue

Thread

Pencil

Scissors

Remember to decorate both sides of your mobile!

1 Draw a picture using different pieces of colored poster board. For example, draw a cat on one poster board and stripes on a poster board of a different color.

2 Cut out your drawings.

3 Glue the different pieces of poster board together to make a complete picture.

You can make
interesting mobiles
by joining
segments
together
with
thread.

4

Make a hole at the top of
your picture. Then tie a piece of
thread to it to make your mobile.

Top Tip

Try making a zigzag fold
on your mobile. This will
help it catch the wind.

Dancing Puppet

You need

White poster board

String

Water

Tape

Scissors

Paint

Brush

Pencil

1 Draw a head, body, arms, and legs on the poster board.

2 Color the pieces and cut them out.

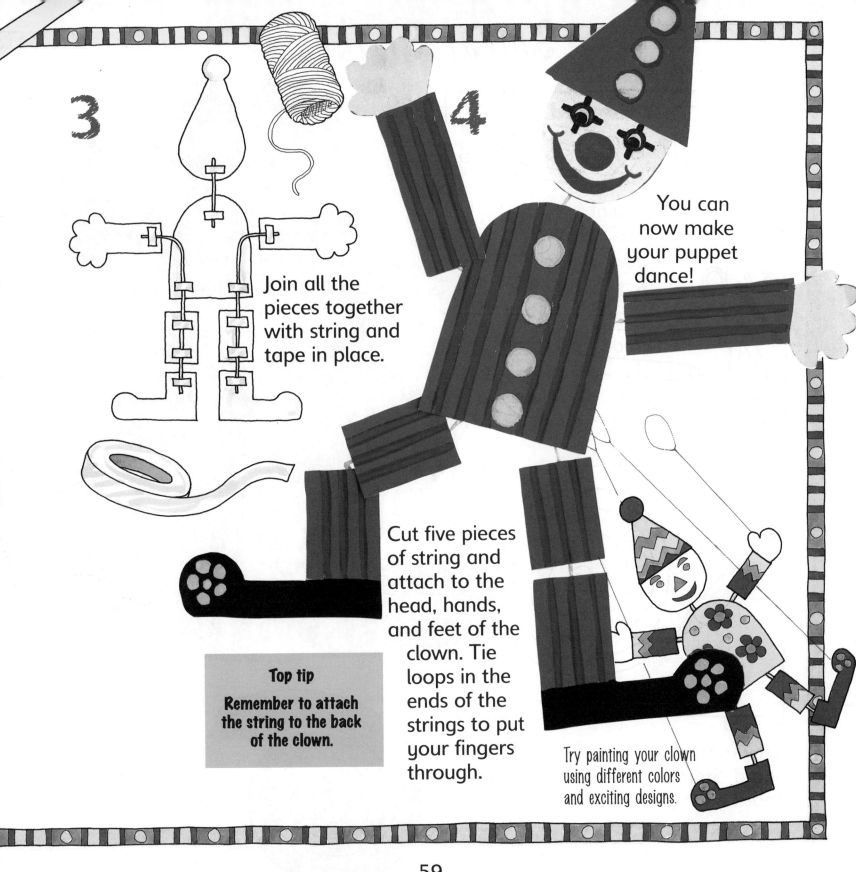

3

Join all the pieces together with string and tape in place.

4

You can now make your puppet dance!

Cut five pieces of string and attach to the head, hands, and feet of the clown. Tie loops in the ends of the strings to put your fingers through.

Top tip

Remember to attach the string to the back of the clown.

Try painting your clown using different colors and exciting designs.

Spiral Snakes

You need

Poster board

Paint

Brush

Scissors

Thread

Pencil

Water

1

Draw a spiral on a piece of poster board. Start at the center of the poster board and work out toward the edge.

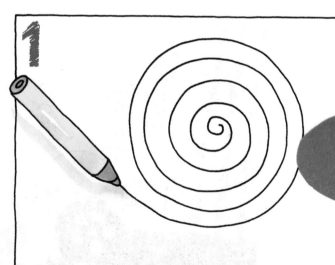

Try painting your snake different colors!

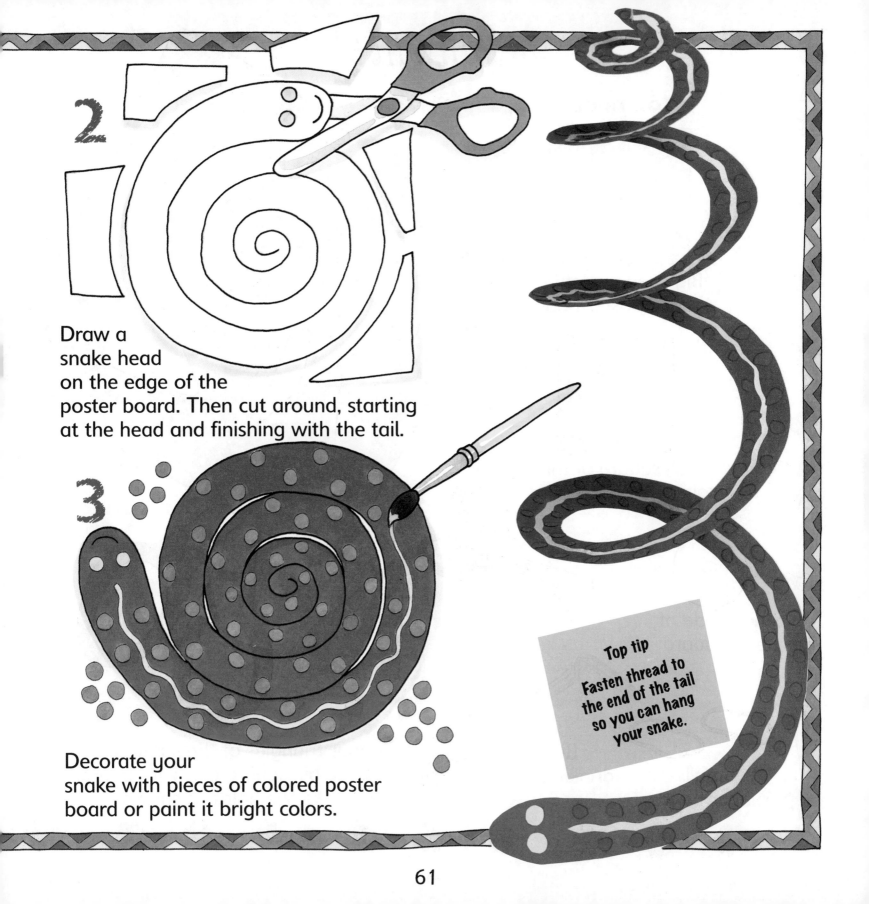

2

Draw a
snake head
on the edge of the
poster board. Then cut around, starting
at the head and finishing with the tail.

3

Decorate your
snake with pieces of colored poster
board or paint it bright colors.

Top tip

Fasten thread to
the end of the tail
so you can hang
your snake.

Pinwheel

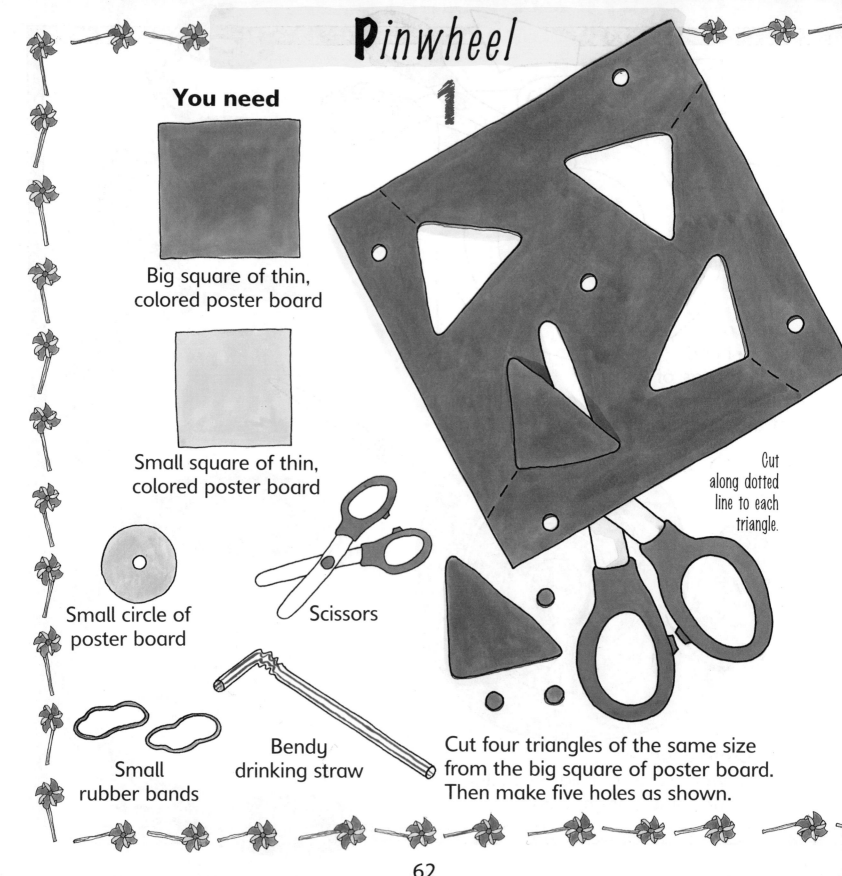

You need

Big square of thin, colored poster board

Small square of thin, colored poster board

Small circle of poster board

Scissors

Small rubber bands

Bendy drinking straw

1

Cut along dotted line to each triangle.

Cut four triangles of the same size from the big square of poster board. Then make five holes as shown.

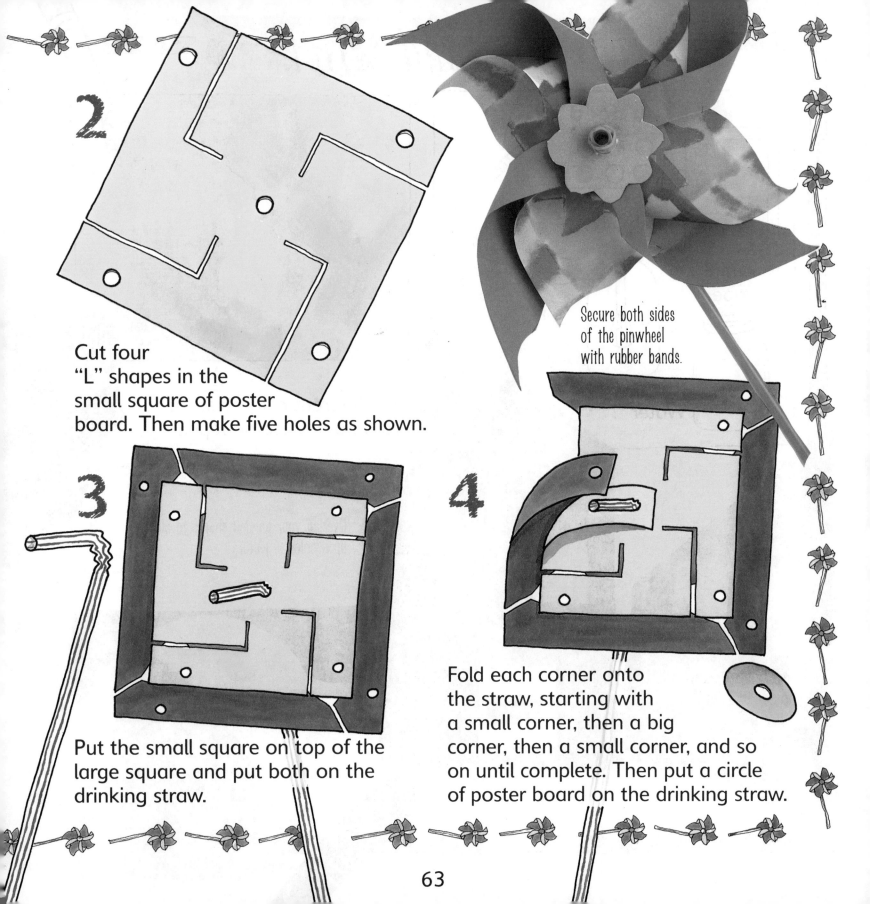

2

Cut four "L" shapes in the small square of poster board. Then make five holes as shown.

Secure both sides of the pinwheel with rubber bands.

3

Put the small square on top of the large square and put both on the drinking straw.

4

Fold each corner onto the straw, starting with a small corner, then a big corner, then a small corner, and so on until complete. Then put a circle of poster board on the drinking straw.

Paint and Stick

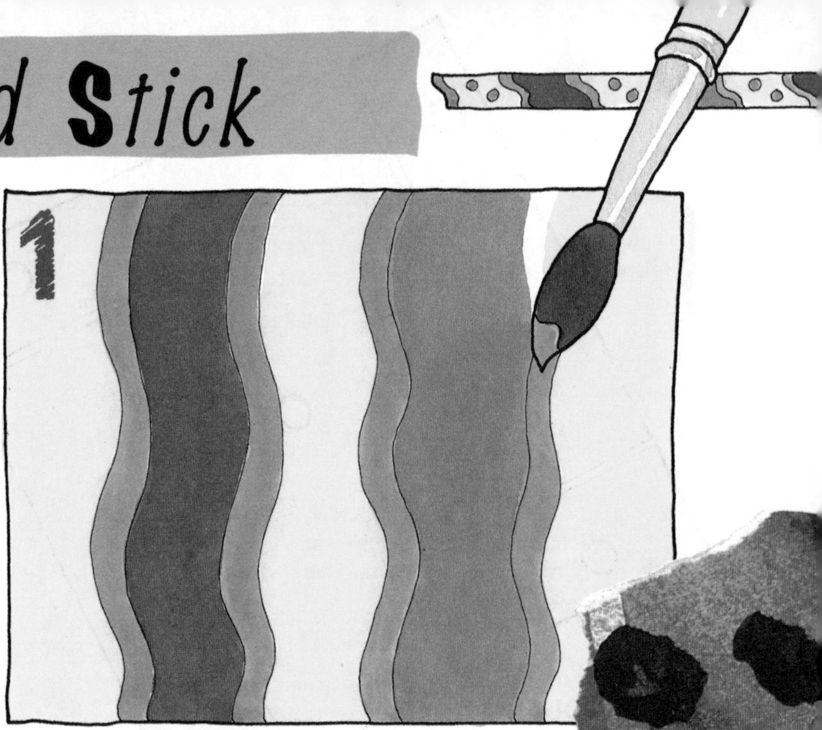

You need

Paint

Brush

White paper

Glue

Scissors

Water

1

Paint different colored stripes across your piece of paper.

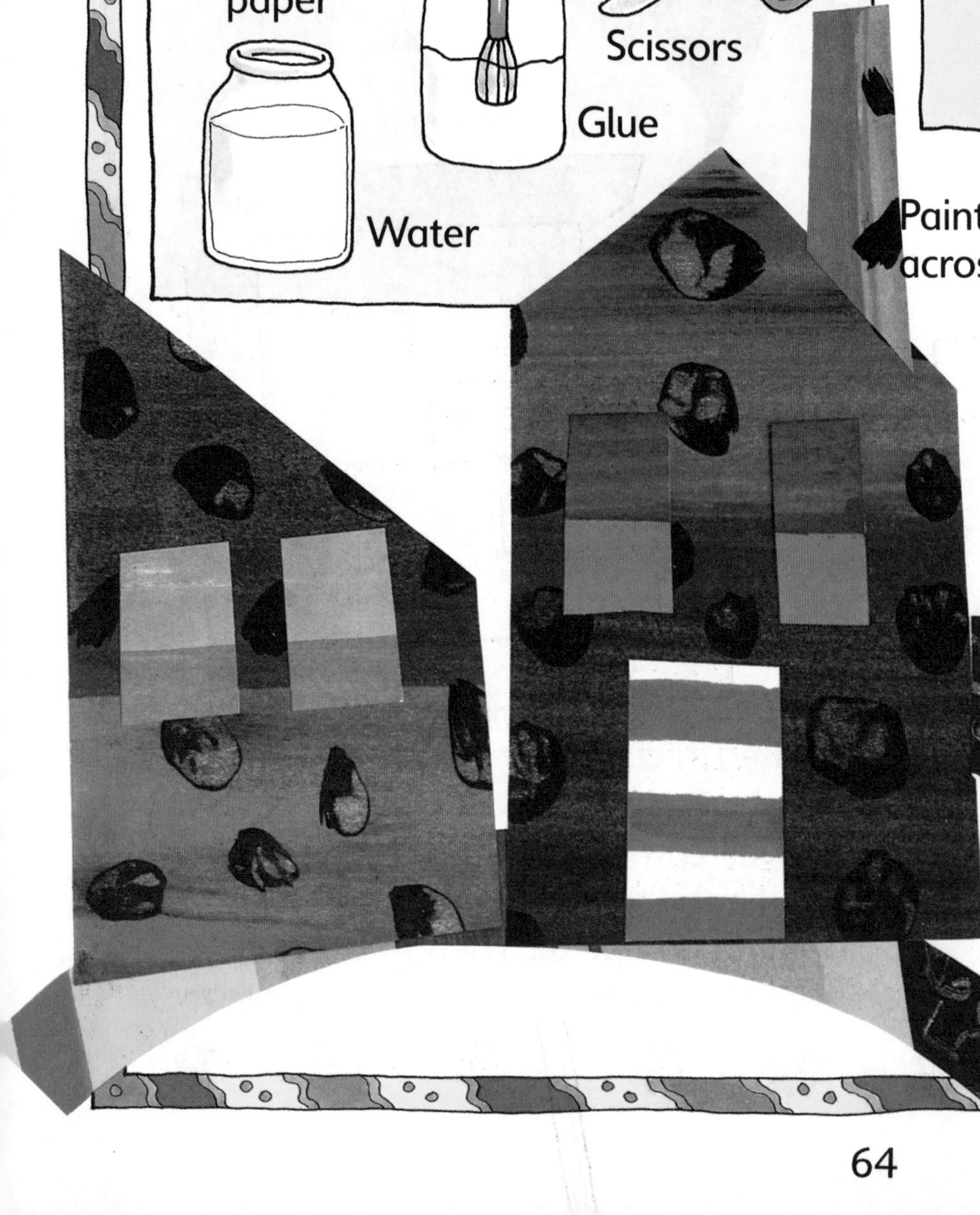

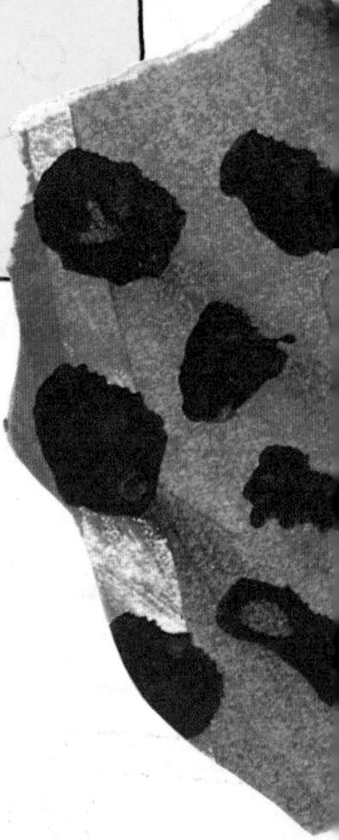

Overlap your painted shapes to build up a colorful picture.

2

When the paint is dry, cut the paper into different sized shapes, such as squares or curves.

3

See how many funny pictures you can make!

Glue the pieces of painted paper on a fresh piece of paper to make a picture.

Top tip
Try painting dots or squiggles on your striped paper to make a more exciting design!

Silhouettes

You need

Colored paper

Scissors

Pencil

Glue

1
Draw a picture on a piece of paper.

2
Cut out the picture.

66

3

Glue it on
a different piece
of paper. Contrasting
colors work best.

Top Tip
Simple pictures drawn on black
paper work best. Orange paper
looks very effective as a
nighttime background.

Pop-up Card

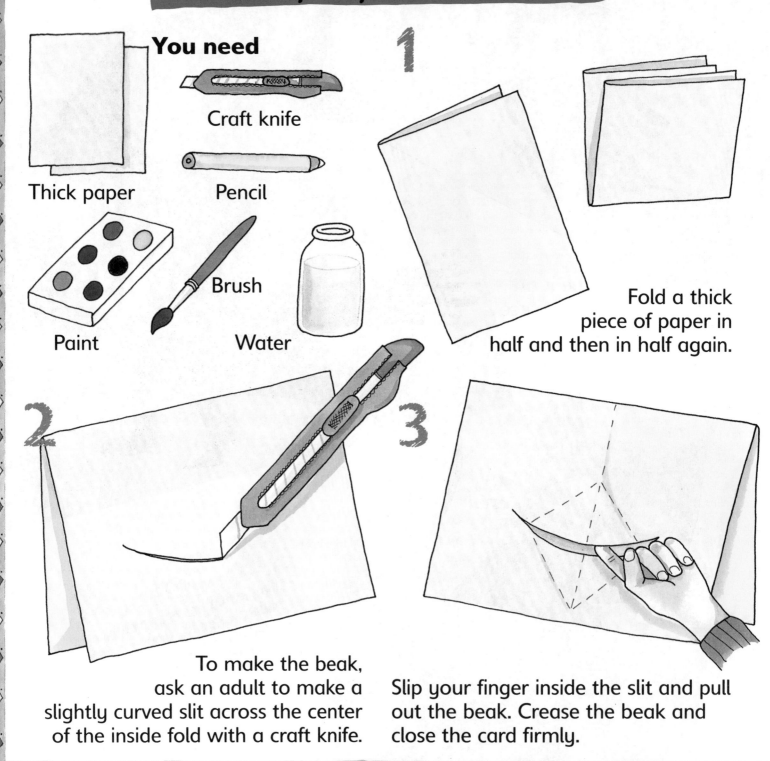

You need

Thick paper

Craft knife

Pencil

Paint

Brush

Water

1

Fold a thick piece of paper in half and then in half again.

2

To make the beak, ask an adult to make a slightly curved slit across the center of the inside fold with a craft knife.

3

Slip your finger inside the slit and pull out the beak. Crease the beak and close the card firmly.

4

Paint the inside of the bird's mouth. Then draw the rest of the bird's head and paint this too.

Top tip
Instead of painting your pop-up card, you could try gluing on different shapes made out of colored paper.

Puppet Theater

You need

Shoebox

Scissors

Brush

Glue

Paint

Water

Old magazines

Poster board

Drinking straws

Tape

1

Paint the box bright colors.

Ask an adult to cut two slits in both ends of the shoebox.

2

Choose a good backdrop scene from a magazine and glue it on the back of the inside of the box.

70

3

Stick drinking straws on the backs of the puppets with tape.

To make your puppets, glue figures from magazines on poster board and cut them out.

Push the puppets through the slits in the side of the box. You can then move them around to make your own puppet show.

More Ideas

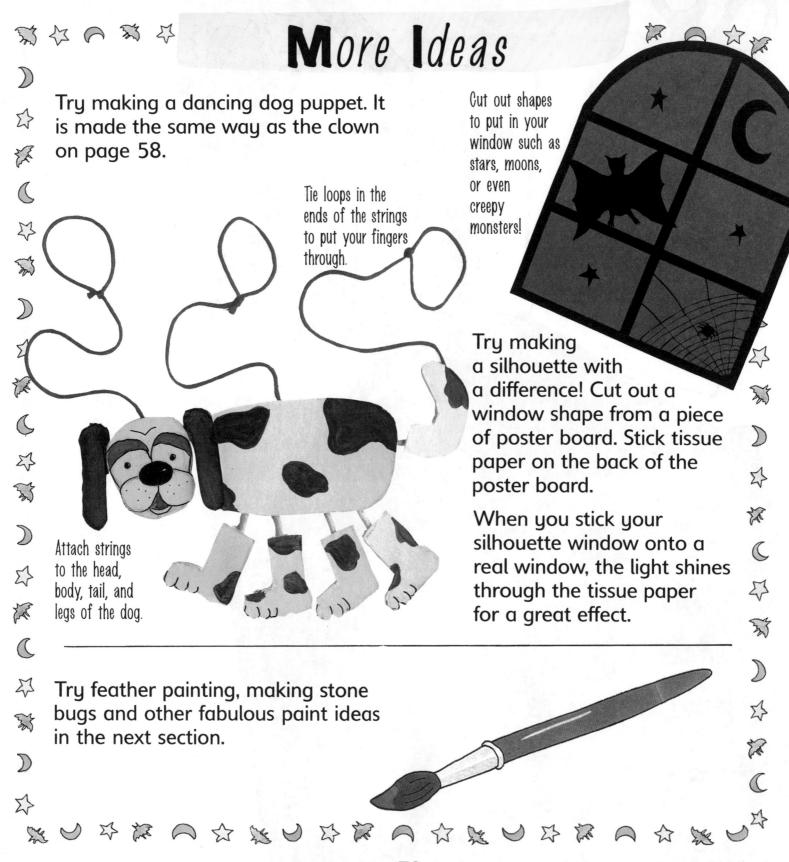

Try making a dancing dog puppet. It is made the same way as the clown on page 58.

Tie loops in the ends of the strings to put your fingers through.

Cut out shapes to put in your window such as stars, moons, or even creepy monsters!

Attach strings to the head, body, tail, and legs of the dog.

Try making a silhouette with a difference! Cut out a window shape from a piece of poster board. Stick tissue paper on the back of the poster board.

When you stick your silhouette window onto a real window, the light shines through the tissue paper for a great effect.

Try feather painting, making stone bugs and other fabulous paint ideas in the next section.

paint

Contents

Hints and Tips

Most of the projects may be made with watercolor <u>or</u> poster paint; a few require poster paint.

When using paint in block form, first drop water onto the paint block and let it soften.

Scrap paper is very useful for trying out your ideas before painting your final picture.

You can buy colored paper from craft shops. Try out your ideas on different types of paper and see the different results you get.

Collect objects such as cartons, foil, board, and string. Keep them together in a useful box, ready for when you need them.

When using powder paint, always add water to the powder (not the powder to water) to make a smooth paint.

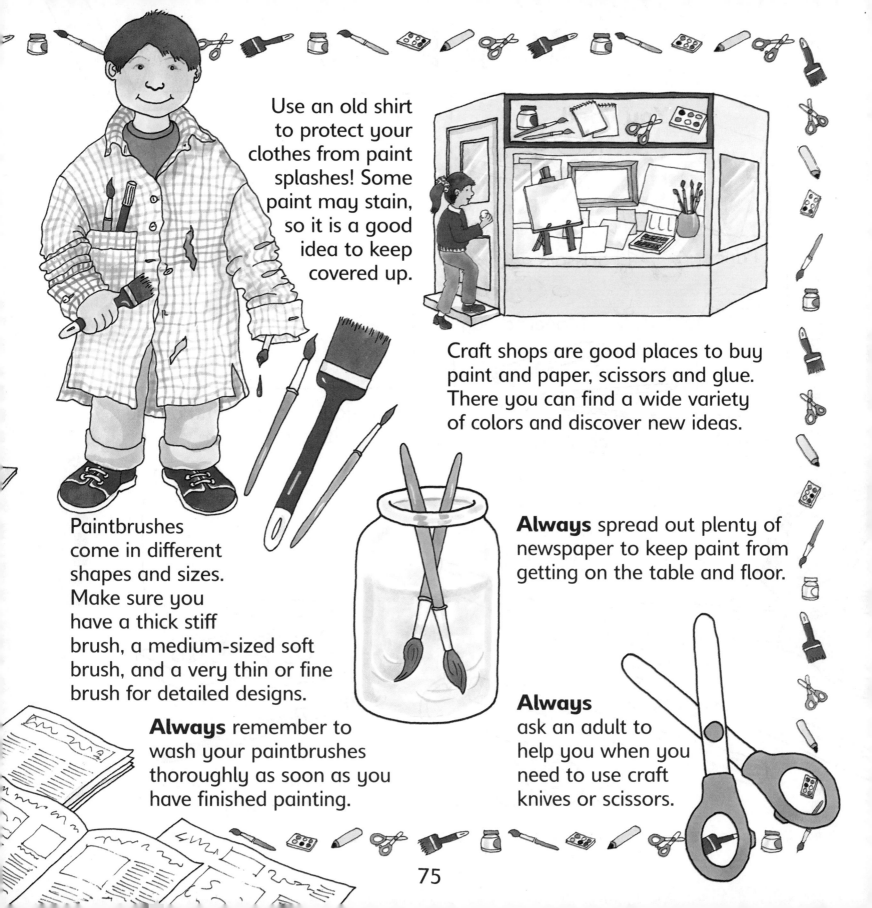

Use an old shirt to protect your clothes from paint splashes! Some paint may stain, so it is a good idea to keep covered up.

Craft shops are good places to buy paint and paper, scissors and glue. There you can find a wide variety of colors and discover new ideas.

Paintbrushes come in different shapes and sizes. Make sure you have a thick stiff brush, a medium-sized soft brush, and a very thin or fine brush for detailed designs.

Always spread out plenty of newspaper to keep paint from getting on the table and floor.

Always remember to wash your paintbrushes thoroughly as soon as you have finished painting.

Always ask an adult to help you when you need to use craft knives or scissors.

Straw Painting

You need

Paper

Paint

Scissors

Modeling clay

Pencil

Water

Drinking straws

1 Draw your design lightly on the paper with a pencil.

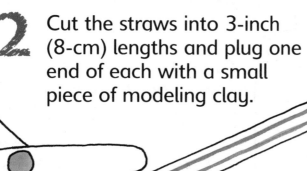

2 Cut the straws into 3-inch (8-cm) lengths and plug one end of each with a small piece of modeling clay.

3 Mix your paint with a little water to make a thin solution.

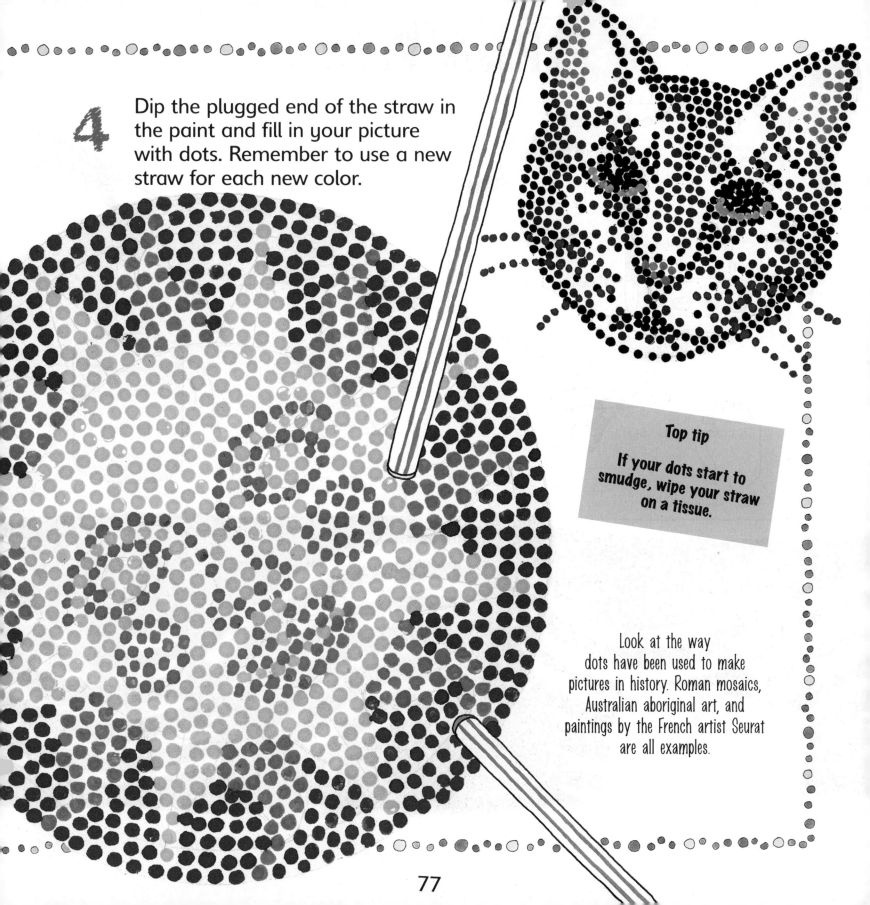

4 Dip the plugged end of the straw in the paint and fill in your picture with dots. Remember to use a new straw for each new color.

Top tip

If your dots start to smudge, wipe your straw on a tissue.

Look at the way dots have been used to make pictures in history. Roman mosaics, Australian aboriginal art, and paintings by the French artist Seurat are all examples.

Paste Paint

You need

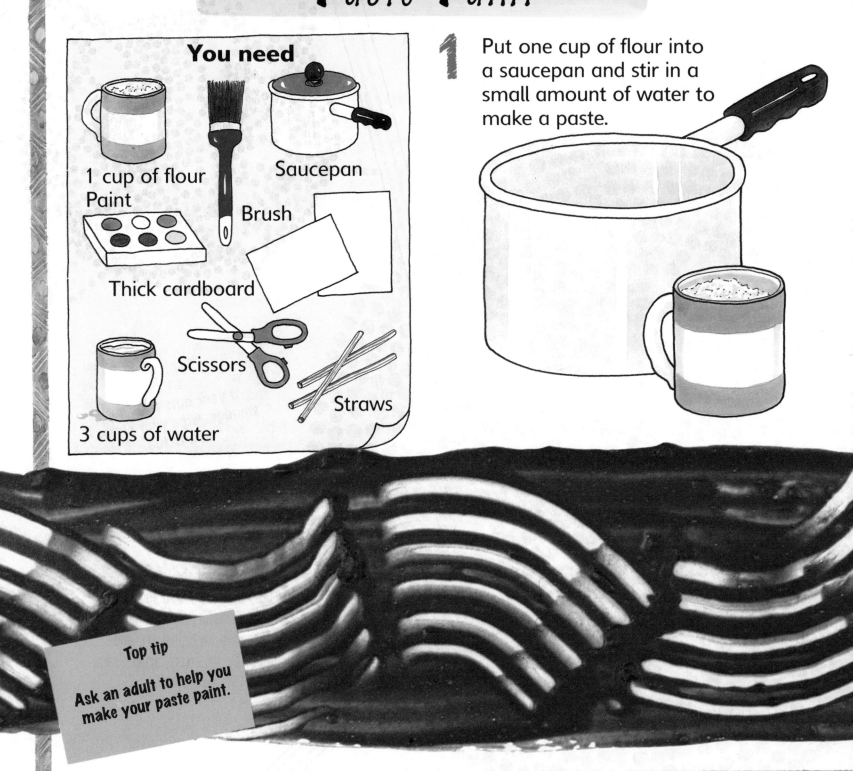

1 cup of flour

Paint

Brush

Saucepan

Thick cardboard

Scissors

Straws

3 cups of water

1 Put one cup of flour into a saucepan and stir in a small amount of water to make a paste.

Top tip

Ask an adult to help you make your paste paint.

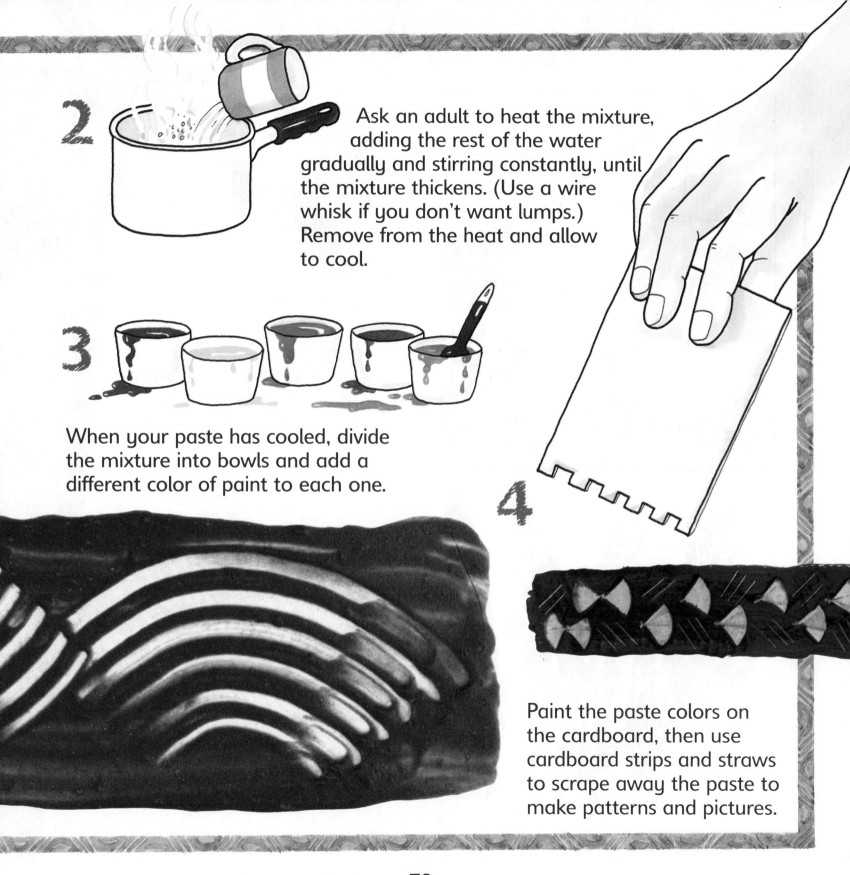

2 Ask an adult to heat the mixture, adding the rest of the water gradually and stirring constantly, until the mixture thickens. (Use a wire whisk if you don't want lumps.) Remove from the heat and allow to cool.

3 When your paste has cooled, divide the mixture into bowls and add a different color of paint to each one.

4 Paint the paste colors on the cardboard, then use cardboard strips and straws to scrape away the paste to make patterns and pictures.

Feather Effect

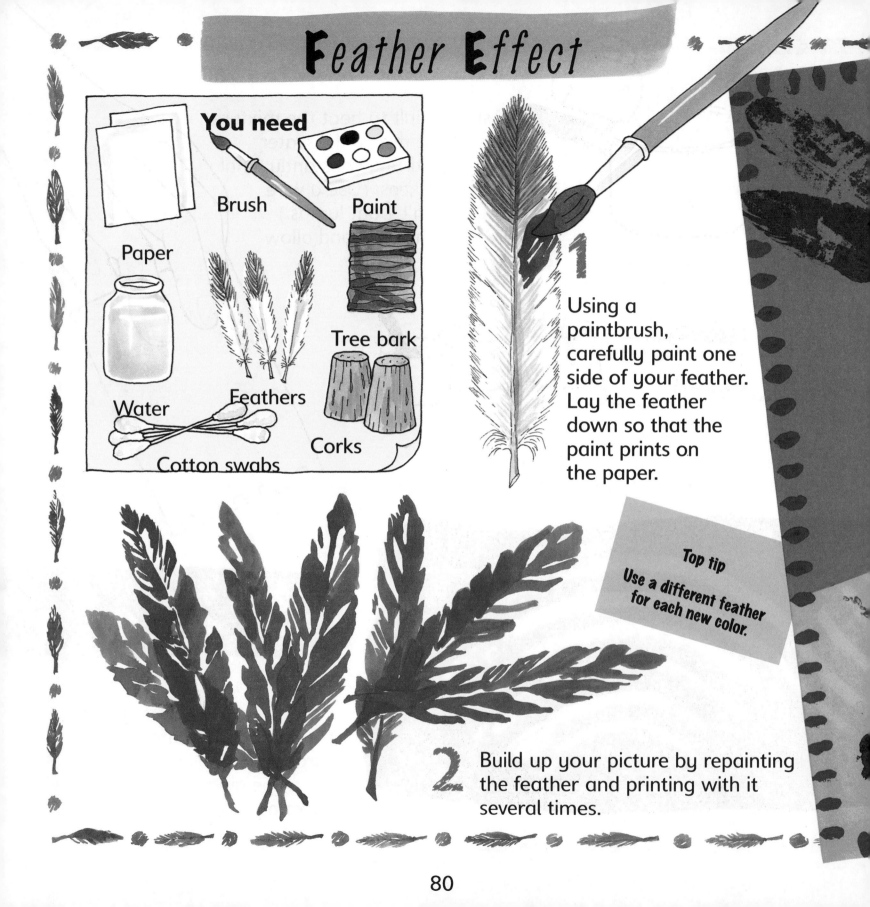

You need

Paper

Brush

Paint

Water

Feathers

Cotton swabs

Tree bark

Corks

1 Using a paintbrush, carefully paint one side of your feather. Lay the feather down so that the paint prints on the paper.

Top tip
Use a different feather for each new color.

2 Build up your picture by repainting the feather and printing with it several times.

3 Use other objects such as tree bark, cotton swabs, and the end of a cork to make different shapes in your picture.

Top tip

Press your feather lightly onto the paper with your finger. Be careful not to move your objects when printing, or they may smudge.

Squeezy Marble

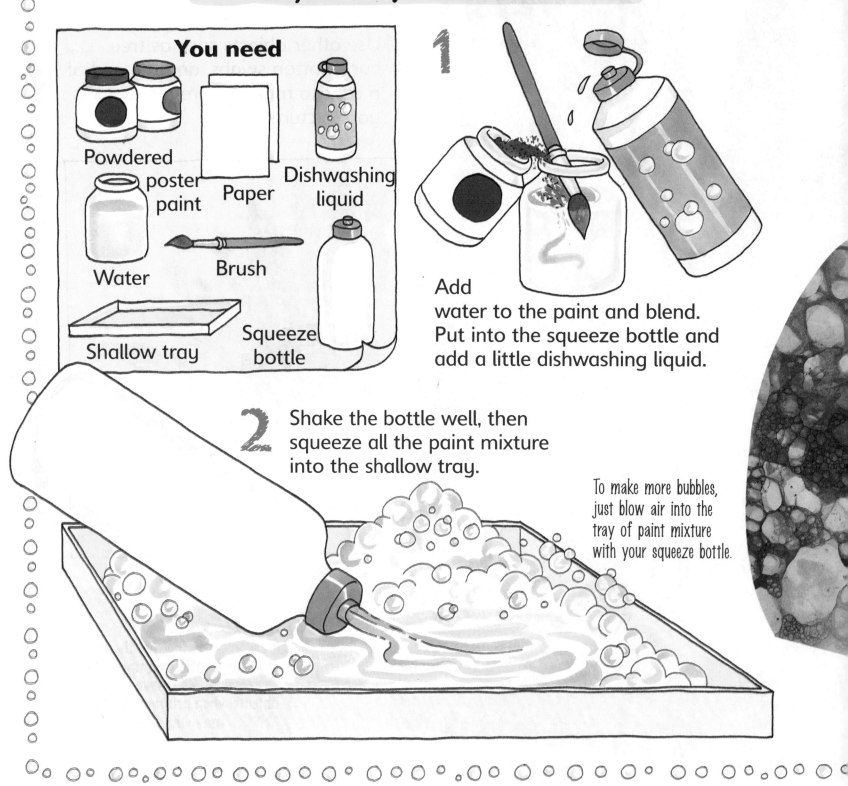

You need

Powdered poster paint

Paper

Dishwashing liquid

Water

Brush

Shallow tray

Squeeze bottle

1 Add water to the paint and blend. Put into the squeeze bottle and add a little dishwashing liquid.

2 Shake the bottle well, then squeeze all the paint mixture into the shallow tray.

To make more bubbles, just blow air into the tray of paint mixture with your squeeze bottle.

3 Quickly place your paper over the colored bubbles and lift it off carefully. Let it dry.

Make colorful pictures with shapes cut from your marbled paper.

Painted Car

You need

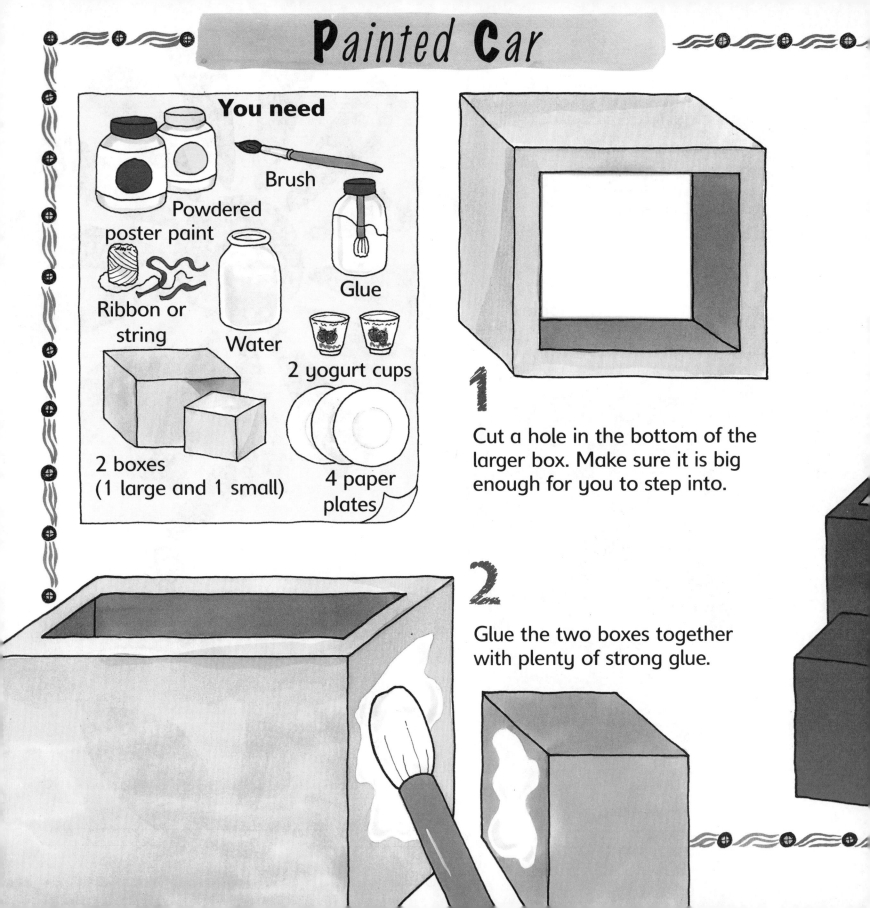

Powdered poster paint

Brush

Glue

Ribbon or string

Water

2 yogurt cups

2 boxes (1 large and 1 small)

4 paper plates

1

Cut a hole in the bottom of the larger box. Make sure it is big enough for you to step into.

2

Glue the two boxes together with plenty of strong glue.

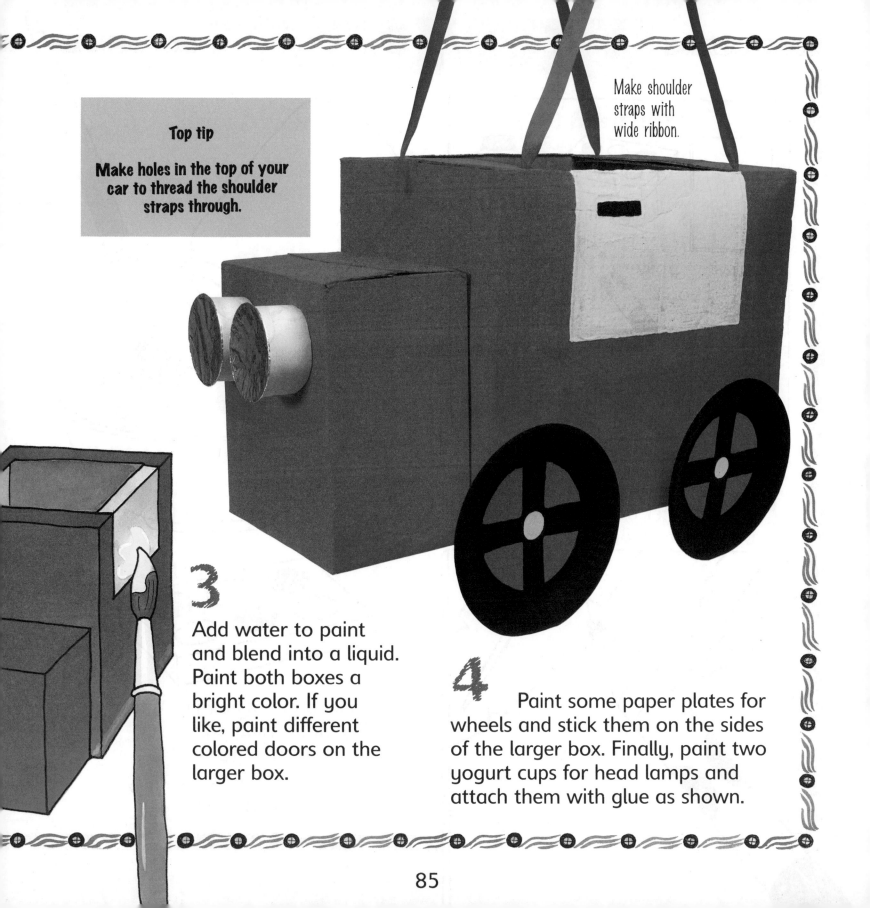

Make shoulder straps with wide ribbon.

Top tip

Make holes in the top of your car to thread the shoulder straps through.

3

Add water to paint and blend into a liquid. Paint both boxes a bright color. If you like, paint different colored doors on the larger box.

4

Paint some paper plates for wheels and stick them on the sides of the larger box. Finally, paint two yogurt cups for head lamps and attach them with glue as shown.

Texture Paints

You need

Thick white poster board

Paint

Liquid glue

Waterproof marker

Water

Brush

Pencil shavings

1 Draw your picture on the thick white poster board using a black waterproof marker.

2 Mix equal amounts of glue and liquid paint (if using paint in a block form, first soften with water). Now add pencil shavings to make a creamy paste.

3

If needed, add more glue to thicken the paint. Paint on your textured paint mixture with a stiff brush.

Sugar Picture

You need

Paper

Paint

Brushes

Water

Powdered sugar

1 Mix a thin solution of water and powdered sugar. Paint a piece of paper with the solution, covering it completely.

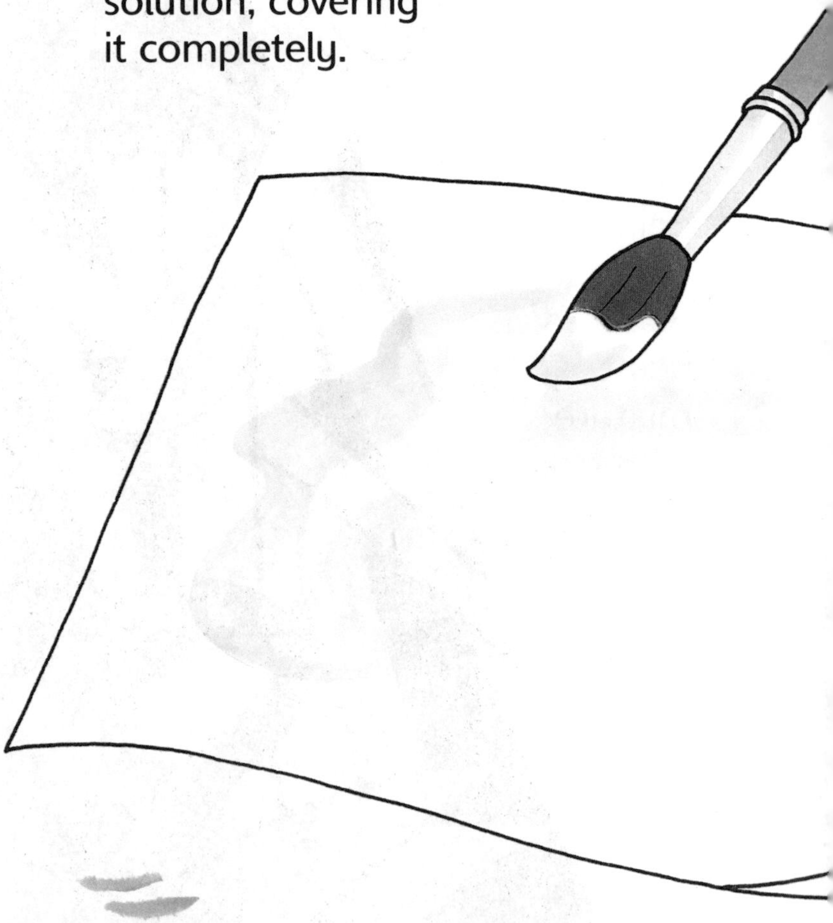

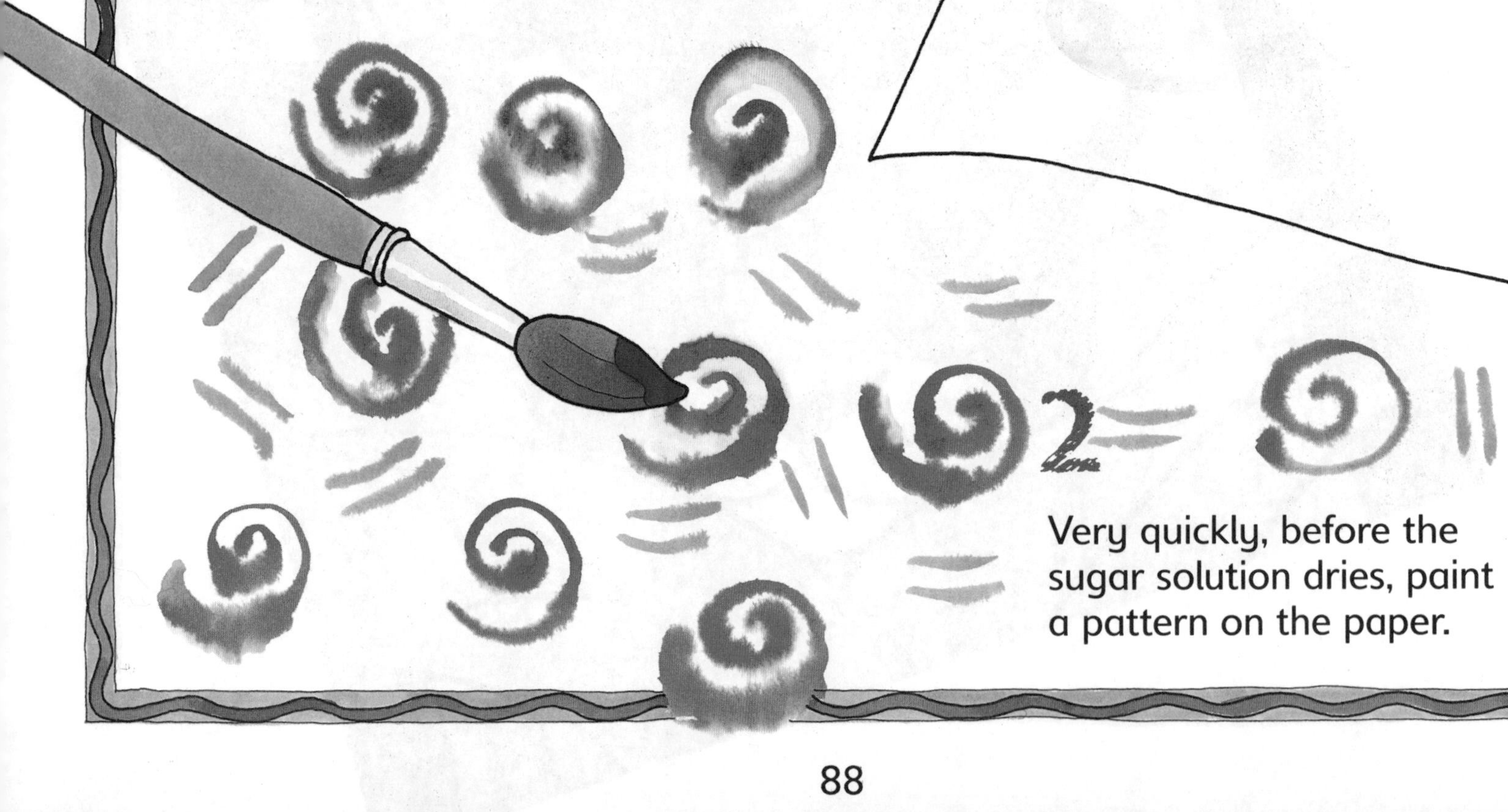

2 Very quickly, before the sugar solution dries, paint a pattern on the paper.

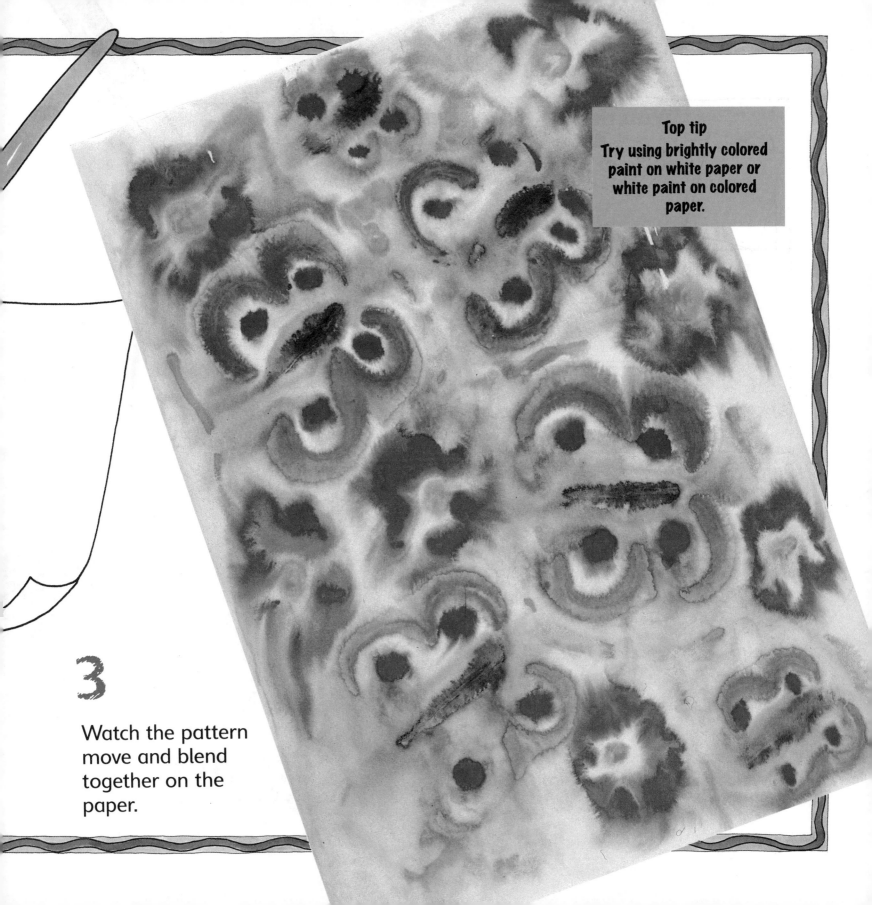

Top tip
Try using brightly colored paint on white paper or white paint on colored paper.

3

Watch the pattern move and blend together on the paper.

Paint Prints

You need

Paper

Paint

Brush

Bubble wrap

Water

Plastic wrap

Paint plenty of color straight on the plastic wrap or bubble wrap.

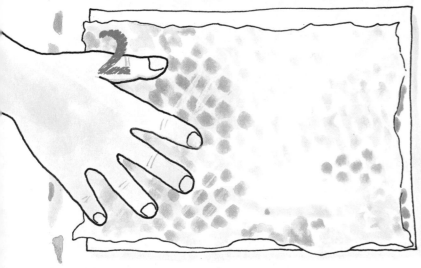

While the paint is still wet, place the plastic wrap or bubble wrap paint side down on your paper.

Leave the wrinkles in the plastic wrap – they will make an interesting pattern.

Top tip

Try using different colors on the same paper. They will blend to make new colors.

Top tip

Add some extra detail by using shiny leaves (such as ivy leaves) in the same way as you used the bubble wrap. You could even wrap the leaves in plastic wrap to give a special effect.

3

Leave the plastic wrap and bubble wrap on the paper until the paint is dry. Then remove it very carefully.

Sponging

You need

Paper

Paint

Brush

Sponges

Scissors

Pen

Water

An old bath sponge works well.

1 Draw shapes on the surface of the sponge using a pen and cut around them carefully.

Top tip

Cut simple shapes – they work best.

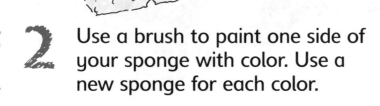

2 Use a brush to paint one side of your sponge with color. Use a new sponge for each color.

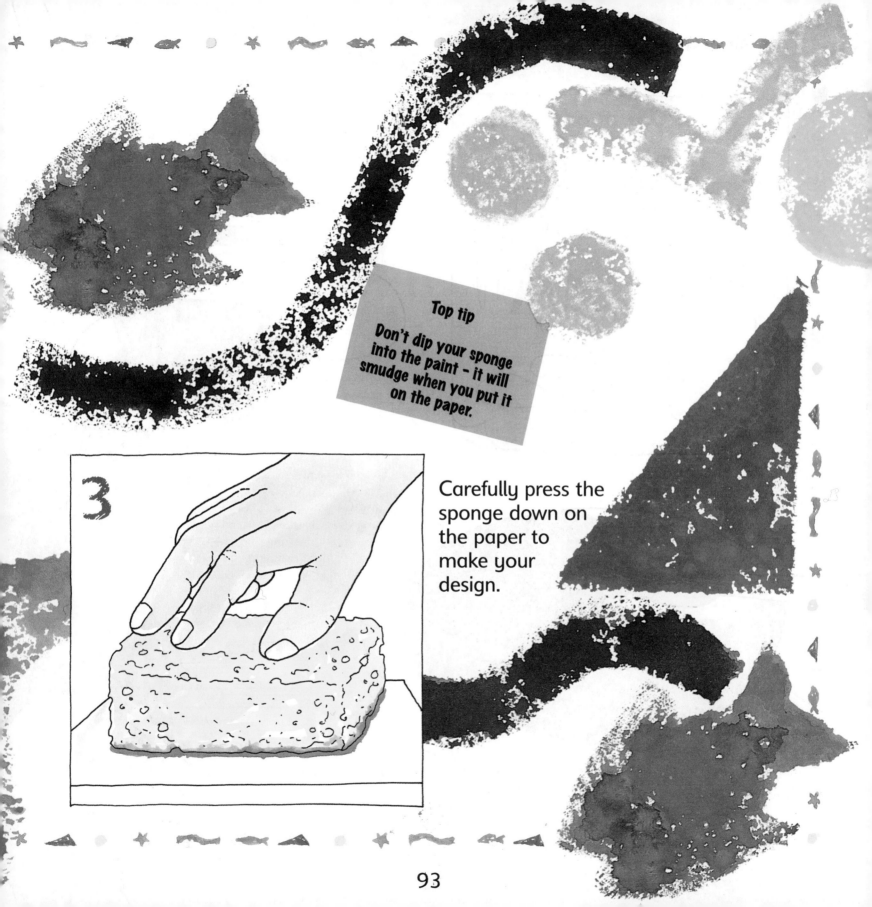

Top tip

Don't dip your sponge into the paint – it will smudge when you put it on the paper.

Carefully press the sponge down on the paper to make your design.

Stone Bugs

You need

Poster paint

Brushes

Water

Stones

1 Use thick poster paint to cover the whole stone. Let it dry, making sure it is resting on its base.

Top tip

Make sure your stones are clean and dry before you start painting.

2 Paint the bottom half of the stone black and let it dry.

3 Now add face, wings, and spots to your bug using a thin paintbrush.

Top tip

Allow each coat of paint to dry thoroughly before adding a new one.

1 Mix equal amounts of paint and liquid glue together.

Use this mixture to paint your design on a piece of poster board.

2 Sprinkle sugar on the wet paint and let it dry.

Try using silver or gold paint for a special sparkly effect.

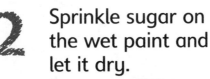

3

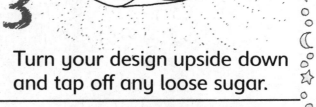

Turn your design upside down and tap off any loose sugar.

Produced by
Zigzag Publishing, a division of
Quadrillion Publishing Ltd.
Godalming Business Centre, Woolsack
Way, Godalming, Surrey GU7 1XW

Distributed in the U.S. by
SMITHMARK PUBLISHERS a division of
U.S. Media Holdings, Inc. 16 East 32nd
Street, New York, NY 10016

Series Concept: Tony Potter
Series Editor: Paul Harrison
Production: Zoë Fawcett
Cover design: Nicky Chapman
Ideas by Sue Clearly, Lisa Nutt,
Pat Thornton, Judy Lewis,
Georgina Fenn, and Sue Partington
Photography: Zul Mukhida

Colour separations: Sussex Repro, England
Printed in France

Copyright © 1996 Zigzag Publishing.
This edition printed in 1997.

Ref: 8372

ISBN 0-7651-9323-X